Praise for Bill Wagner and *The Entrepreneur Next Door*

For anyone who aspires to the challenges of entrepreneurship, this book is a must read. It is the most comprehensive and useful source on the personality, capabilities, and actions required to achieve entrepreneurship success.

-MARK EDWARDS, PH.D., PROFESSOR, STRATEGIC MARKETING AND ENTREPRENEURSHIP,
ARIZONA STATE UNIVERSITY AND CEO OF TALENTDNA

Bill Wagner's timing is perfect. Opportunities abound for entrepreneurs today, and The Entrepreneur Next Door *arrives just in time. Whether you're a born businessperson or what Bill calls a "wantrepreneur," this book gives you a step-by-step blueprint for success. Thank you, Bill, for disproving the adage that only some people can be great entrepreneurs.*

-RAFAEL PASTOR, CHAIRMAN OF THE BOARD AND CEO, VISTAGE INTERNATIONAL

I never thought that a book entitled The Entrepreneur Next Door *would attract my attention, let alone keep it. I like the approach of starting with a deep personal analysis – a sense of self, and then moving on from there. These points of contact are content hooks that pulled me along in the process of seeing where I fit in. Especially interesting is the ability to see exactly where you are. This is a book for the doubters and nay-sayers. It's a conversion experience!*

-MICHAEL T. HILLER, VICE PRESIDENT ADMINISTRATION, STANFORD FEDERAL CREDIT UNION

Bill Wagner has an uncanny, objective understanding of the dynamics of the workplace environment and in this engaging and humorous book he shares his insights, candor and ability to take a complex subject such as personality and bring it to life and make it understandable.

-MATTHEW SHAY, PRESIDENT 2006, INTERNATIONAL FRANCHISE ASSOCIATION

The Entrepreneur Next Door *is a must read for anyone considering a future in franchising. While I was at* It's A Grind Coffee House, *we were always looking for an entrepreneur with the ideal personality for our business. They are more successful, achieve greater growth sooner, and are certainly more enjoyable to work with. Bill's Five Tier Performance Pyramid is one of the best cognitive processes I have seen in managing the growth of our franchisees.* The Entrepreneur Next Door *truly brings it home and the reader with it. It works! Read it, learn and get ready to grow.*

-STEVE OLSON, PUBLISHER, FRANCHISE UPDATE MEDIA GROUP

The information found in The Entrepreneur Next Door *will take any person regardless of their background to new heights in their personal and professional development. From struggling business owners to the salesperson on the street, the useful and practical strategies offered by Bill Wagner should be at the top of everyone's "must read" list, especially if they are serious about being successful. If you and your company want to do more, be more, and have more, then* The Entrepreneur Next Door *will take you to the next level and beyond.*

-CHUCK BAUER, SALES COACH, DALLAS TEXAS

Congratulations on your book; it is a major effort that will certainly cement your reputation in the world of entrepreneurial scholarship! I appreciate having the opportunity to read this great academic work! Best of luck for a blockbuster success!

-GORDON LOGAN, CEO, SPORTS CLIPS, INC.

Bill has an amazing ability to disarm type-A executives. His book helped me and my colleagues learn how to use our natural strengths to become better leaders, better spouses, better parents and better people! I learned how to use my strengths to deliver better service and develop a more profitable company.

-KIM ELLIS, SENIOR CONSULTANT, MICHAEL SEID & ASSOCIATES, LLC

Bill Wagner came to our facility and conducted a full day retreat. My goal was to understand how my site managers think and process through the Leadership 360 process. We received so much more than that! It was truly a game-changing experience for me and my team. When it comes to providing helpful insight to various behavioral and character traits, Bill Wagner has been able to provide invaluable assistance to our business.

-WENDY KARSTEN, CEO, HUNTINGTON MEDICAL FOUNDATION

Bill Wagner has unique insights into the characteristics and behaviors of entrepreneurs. Are certain people better 'wired' for succeeding in business than others? Bill Wagner seems to know.

-JOE MATTHEWS, FRANCHISE PERFORMANCE GROUP, CO-AUTHOR OF *STREET SMART FRANCHISING*

In my opinion, Bill's involvement has been a key factor in our continued growth and success.

-ADAM L. EISEMAN, CEO, THE LLOYD GROUP

In a graduate school of business, we cover an enormous number of topics. I wish we had a class solely to learn and understand the impact of one's personality on their ultimate choice of endeavor and success. Your content is one of the most useful and long-reaching messages my students have had.

-KATE MCKEOWN, PROFESSOR, ENTREPRENEUR, FORDHAM UNIVERSITY

You have contributed greatly to the growth and education of our YEO membership. Rarely have I worked with a company that provides so much. Your presentations at all YEO's International Conferences and universities always receive extremely high ratings and your exceptional knowledge provides our members with valuable take-home value.

-RICHARD BRIGHT, MARKETING AND COMMUNICATIONS DIRECTOR, YOUNG ENTREPRENEURS' ORGANIZATION (YEO)

In a world where everyone seems to be plugging their latest and greatest "behavioral assessments" and "franchise owner opinion surveys," Bill Wagner's company is one of the few that actually delivers! In less than one year, they have become one of our key strategic partners. Their unique product mix – coupled with outstanding service and support, has had a discernible impact on our bottom line.

-RICK BASCH, VICE PRESIDENT, THE LITTLE GYM INTERNATIONAL

Bill has given us great insight into how different characteristics perform and helped us assess what kinds of people are better suited in each kind of unique job-related roles. Embracing Bill's systems is a rock-solid investment.

-JEFF WALKER, CEO, SUPER D/PHANTOM DISTRIBUTION

You helped our members to anticipate company growth issues and look realistically at the future of their businesses. More importantly, you created an understanding of how their own behaviors and actions affect their personal growth potential.

-ROBERT S. MORGAN, PRESIDENT COUNCIL OF GROWING COMPANIES

In a world where everyone seems to be plugging their latest and greatest, Bill Wagner and his team at Accord Management Systems deliver. We now understand what makes our employees and franchise owners tick and are therefore able to create custom-tailored solutions to meet everyone's needs.

-RICK BASCH, VICE PRESIDENT, SYNERGY HOMECARE

Bill Wagner

The

Entrepreneur

Next Door

Getting the People Side of Business Right...

Including Yourself

Cover Design: Kimb Manson Graphic Design

Library of Congress Cataloging-in-Publication Data

      Wagner, Bill.
          The Entrepreneur Next Door/by Bill Wagner.
         p. cm
        ISBN

        1.   Entrepreneurship. 2. Leadership I. Title.
        HB615.W32 2006
        658.02'2-dc22   2006004269

      Printed in the United States

11 10 09 08 07 06   10 9 8 7 6 5 4 3 2 1

Accord Press
Second Edition

Contents

List of Figures

Dedication

Authors feel that a book's dedication is one of the most thought-provoking aspects of completing a book. This is, however, the easiest. I have been gifted with an absolutely wonderful and supportive family. I would not be successful today without my wife, Renee. She is my dearest friend and provides me with my life's balance. It is Renee's continued guidance and belief in my abilities that has allowed this work (pleasure) to take form. While I am blessed with street smarts, Renee has the intellect. (She is the one with the Doctorate of Education.)

Renee and I share three wonderful children. At this writing our oldest, Alex, an independent filmmaker in NYC, is driven and creative and is putting the final touches on her first documentary. Rebecca, "Daddy's Little Girl," is a junior at Bard College in New York. She has already surpassed my abilities in both math and science. Her advantage is that she also possesses a fully developed right brain and has creativity as well. She has the best sense of humor (mine) and brings me both joy and challenge. She is still a teen. Josh is a senior at Westlake High School and studying to become a pilot. He has successfully soloed, which of course is so much better than unsuccessfully soloing. He is sifting through his college acceptances to determine his college of choice. Sometimes we have motivation enough in life to make our way; I find my family to be my guiding light, without which there would be no book and perhaps no "me."

I have always stressed the importance of reading. As children we learn to read and, later, we read to learn. Let this work be our children's legacy of learning.

Bill Wagner

Words of Gratitude

IT WAS THE MCQUAIG SYSTEM™ that I chose to measure the personalities of our entrepreneurs. The McQuaig Institute is a leader in the field of psychometric use and application. I reviewed more than 20 different instruments before choosing the McQuaig System. It's simply the best.

A special thank you to my mother-in-law, Blanche Salick, who some 20-plus years ago made an investment in me, both financial and motivational. Sadly, she passed away this past year at the age of 100.

Al Hazan has been my TEC Chair (The Executive Committee, now Vistage) for the past 10 years. It has been his mission to teach me how to be a better leader. I have fought him every step of the way. It is largely through his efforts that I am succeeding. I have learned that it is easier to listen than deal with his wrath.

The co-founders of Plumeus, Vratislav Jerabek and Ilona Jerabek, are two of the most brilliant entrepreneurs I have been fortunate enough to work with. They are the creators and providers of more than 100 online assessments. When you take one of our online tests at www.theentrepreneurnextdoor.com, it will be their handiwork you are enjoying.

The Entrepreneurs Organization (EO) allowed me access to its members and was instrumental in the research for this project. For those of you who haven't figured it out yet, EO is the premier learning organization for young entrepreneurs.

Vistage 511 was my Vistage group that Al Hazan chaired. Its members have been instrumental in my growth and development. They are: Chris Brown, Howard Davis, Mike McMaster, Art Nakagawa, Paul Revlin, Frank Spaeth and Rudi Weinberg.

My book agent, Jeff Herman, of the Jeff Herman Literary Agency, LLC.

My dedicated staff, which includes Kim Caputo. Her primary job is to keep me focused and keep my company running. Without her, I would surely perish. Tom Welz, Business Development guru extraordinaire. Lisa Borghei, who keeps our projects on task and the money coming in. And Amanda Harris, who is one loyal, warm, and dedicated individual.

Create Your Own
Declaration of Independence
by Jeffrey Gitomer

LOOKING FOR REAL INCOME? What are you doing about it?

I started selling candy bars door to door when I was seven years old. I thought it would be a good idea to raise money for charity, buying candy bars for a nickel and selling them for a dime. I raised about $15 and gave all the money to charity, not realizing I was supposed to keep my costs, so I could do it again. Entrepreneurial success and failure at the same time.

Everyone remembers their first entrepreneurial experience. It might have been a school fundraiser, Junior Achievement, or working at an early age in your family's business. Chances are, that's when the questions, "Do I like this? Is this for me? Is it fun?" started drifting through your mind. If you have an entrepreneurial spirit, those questions stay with you as you enter the working world. And so do the choices – working for someone else or working for yourself.

I had the entrepreneurial urge at an early age and it stayed with me my entire life. When did it hit you? What have you done about it so far?

Some people have the entrepreneurial spirit in their blood. Others try to acquire it once they find out that working class America is not for them, or they get laid off, or downsized, or they hate their bosses, or they're not making the kind of money they'd like to (or need to) make.

The American Dream is available for anyone who decides to reach for the brass ring. Most people have short arms. They may think about it. They may look at others who do it. They may even harbor a secret desire to do it. But they keep their hands in their pockets. The American Dream is only achieved when someone has a strong desire, decides to take a risk, and believes he has the wherewithal to make it happen.

How about you? Are you looking for more? Are you looking to be your own boss? Are you looking to achieve greater wealth? Do you have enough desire and fortitude to turn the dream into a reality?

Hey, the guy next door has done it. So can you!

If you have a spark of entrepreneurial spirit in your soul, this book will not only help you uncover it – it will show you how to use it. Not in a general way, but in a way that is specifically tailored to your personality, which means it gives you the best chance to succeed.

Words of Caution

This is not a book you can read quickly. It's definitely not a "one-size-fits-all." Rather, this is a book that interacts with your thought process, helps you capture and understand your personality and skill set, and then provides working guidance so that you can start a business, build a business, and succeed based on the proven methods and results of others.

Words of Reality

Everyone who succeeds in business seeks guidance. Bill Wagner's book is a built-in mentor. Bill knows entrepreneurs the way I know salespeople – top to bottom, inside and out. Having known Bill personally for years, I can attest to his expertise, his thoroughness, and his firm grip on reality. He is not just a voice of experience, but also a voice of wisdom.

Words of Encouragement

Becoming a successful entrepreneur doesn't have to take long or be as hard as you think. If you find out how to succeed based on your own personality, and you learn how to hire and manage people based on their personalities, you can achieve your goals in half the time, with half the headaches.

The Entrepreneur Next Door is not just a book. It's a blueprint that shows you the step-by-step process for building your own business and creating independence, financial independence, for yourself and those you love.

-Jeffrey Gitomer, author of
The Sales Bible and *The Little Red Book of Selling*

Preface

The Entrepreneur Next Door is based on research and empirical evidence that proves why personality is the most important variable in how and why we succeed or fail as entrepreneurs.

First and foremost, your personality and how well you manage it has a greater impact on your overall business success than do skills, education, knowledge, and experience.

Second, but equally important, hiring the right person for the right job based on personality is one of the most effective ways to ensure your business success. When someone has the right personality for a particular job, the chances of him doing the job well are dramatically increased.

If you don't have the right personality for a particular position, it doesn't preclude your success. But it does make it more challenging and often more stressful. There is a behavioral gap that exists for all of us. It is the difference between the behavioral requirements of our position and our own personality. The closer the gap, the easier the job is to accomplish; the wider the gap, the more energy required to do the job. The question to ask is, "Since I have a choice, what am I most passionate about and what do I most want to do?"

As many very successful entrepreneurs have demonstrated, it's less important to be an expert in the type of business you're running than it is to be an expert at running your business. Starting, running and leading a business are not things that most entrepreneurs studied in school. Today there are hundreds of universities that offer classes in entrepreneurship. Some even offer degrees and masters programs. You are about to receive an education that makes all people-related things...understandable and predictable.

By learning how *your* personality type is most likely to succeed, you can take the fast track to entrepreneurial success. By learning how to hire and manage your employees based on *their* personality types, you're on your way to greater freedom and *Managing Your Gaps*.

The Research Study

Over the course of five years, I surveyed 1,509 entrepreneurs, most of who were under the age of 40 and had annual business revenues exceeding $1 million. The vast majority of my research participants were members of the Young Entrepreneurs Organization (YEO). It's now named EO, Entrepreneurs Organization. Our study group had an average age of 31 and a net worth of $3.1 million.

Each entrepreneur completed a personality survey, emotional intelligence test, and a brain dominance test. They also completed a 160-question survey regarding their backgrounds, experience, education, beliefs, strengths, and challenges.

As I began to review the results, I was intrigued by the grouping of similar traits. I had never anticipated so much strength, power, raw dominance, and ego in one segment of the population. That moment was the beginning of my path to document entrepreneurs' secrets and frustrations – rich and colorful information about my favorite topic, entrepreneurs, and, most importantly, how anyone can become one. In retrospect, it makes sense as we were surveying those that were already successful. Similar to research conducted by Jim Collins of "Good to Great" fame, where he looked at the data points in determining the companies he wanted to include, we studied those that were already successful. We did so in order to determine the common traits that infer entrepreneurial success.

This is Really Important! *Really!!!*

This is the book's second edition. Therefore, we have had the opportunity to look at additional data points and have drawn some very noteworthy conclusions:

1. Those that know, understand, and embrace the behavioral requirements of their position have a greater opportunity to succeed – regardless of their personality.
2. Those whose personality matches the requirements of their position have an even greater opportunity at success.
3. Changing one's behavior to match the job requires cognitive capacity.
4. The more you are forced to change your behaviors, the more energy it requires. If you go home at the end of the day and are tired X number of days per week, think about what you've been doing in those days. You've probably been going against your natural grain or personality.
5. When you're tired or frustrated, just know this is normal for the energy you are burning through. If you don't understand the source of your frustration, you run the risk of allowing it to become bigger than it needs to be.

6. When people don't perform to the capacity of the position, they can create behavioral bottlenecks.
7. When you measure and enforce proper job-fit you create a model of predictability. If you can predict it, you can use it. If it's negative you can prevent it.
8. Knowing and understanding job-fit means you can hire the right person for the right seat on the proverbial bus.
9. With job-fit, you can promote people to positions where they will succeed, and therefore avoid the dreaded Peter Principle.
10. Learn to create organizational health and avoid a level of potential dysfunction.

If you can truly get to know yourself and the innate tendencies of the people who work for you, you can follow the Five-Tier Performance Pyramid I share with my clients and achieve the results you desire. Understanding your personality and your employees' unique personalities is paramount to your success. Personality is Tier I of the Performance Pyramid. It forms the foundation for Tier II: Job Behaviors, Tier III: Actions, Tier IV: Metrics, and Tier V: Results. (See Figure 1.1: The Performance Pyramid - Chapter 1.)

Accuracy

I have made every attempt to ensure that this book's information, data, quotations, and results are completely accurate. If you find a mistake or what you believe is an inaccuracy of any kind, please call Oprah immediately. Actually, if Oprah invites me to appear on her show, I won't be apologizing for inaccuracies. I'll be there to share some of the most profound information that entrepreneurs need in order to succeed and, in their understanding, provide motivating work situations for their employees.

Throughout the course of the book I talk about the Young Entrepreneurs Organization (YEO), which changed its name to Entrepreneurs' Organization (EO), and The Executive Committee (TEC), which is now Vistage International. I refer to them as YEO and TEC or Vistage because those were their names during the time I was conducting my research and writing this book. I, however, have maintained my same name.

Value

My career is based on providing strong take-home value. The vast majority of my clients are entrepreneurs and the only thing they are interested in is results. If you're not convinced by the end of Chapter 1 that your entrepreneurial success can be greatly enhanced by this book, I hope you borrowed the book from the library. I wouldn't want you to say you didn't get your money's worth. But if you are convinced, and you accept the concepts found within my book, then put these ideas into action – now. You're in for the ride of your life!

Note: The use of the pronoun "he" is in no way an inference that this book is for, or about, men alone. "He" is representational of both "he" and "she" and is used simply to avoid the cumbersome "he/she" and "him/her," which tends to distract from the content of the material.

PART

1

Who Is the Entrepreneur Next Door?

CHAPTER

1

Succeeding In Business the First Time

AMERICA IS IN THE MIDST OF AN ENTREPRENEURIAL REVOLUTION. EVERY 45 SECONDS a new business is born. Tragically, two out of three perish before their third birthdays. Yet, despite this stark reality, half the U.S. population entertains the idea of self-employment and 500,000 Americans take the leap every year. Today, there are more than 16 million small businesses operating within the United States.

Through extensive research and testing, my wife Renee and I, co-founders of Accord Management Systems Inc., now know how and why some entrepreneurs become multi-millionaires, others do moderately well, some barely survive and most don't. *The Entrepreneur Next Door* describes the natural entrepreneurial personality types (born leaders), the corporate leaders often referred to as intrapreneurs, and those who would like to be in business but have not had the opportunity, the wherewithal, or perhaps the inclination. I will refer to this last group as "wantrepreneurs." Wantrepreneurs are often successful business owners but not necessarily founders or born leaders. They are able to leverage their strengths and compensate for their limitations.

You'll also find out what happens when entrepreneurs become their own worst enemies. Most entrepreneurs don't achieve the level of success, financial or otherwise, that they dream or scheme about and, not surprisingly, these entrepreneurs have some personality traits in common. This book discusses the pitfalls, potential landmines and behavioral bottlenecks that go hand-in-hand with the various entrepreneurial personalities. It also offers insights for solving these challenges.

For example, consider some very successful and very different entrepreneurs:

- Bill Gates displayed the big-picture thinking necessary for success. He dealt well with ambiguity and figured it out as time went on.
- Steve Jobs had the innovative genius, product and customer-centric understanding to create a phenomenal legacy, despite what some described as his "people challenges."
- Conrad Hilton knew little of the lodging and service industry when he decided to build his first hotel. He had unwavering determination, self-confidence, and a strong belief in himself.
- Herb Kelleher of Southwest Airlines solidified his initial idea by writing it on a napkin. For over 30 years his company has maintained profitability.

These examples are simply a few who made the headlines. There are millions of other successful business leaders and owners that have several things in common: an entrepreneurial or wantrepreneurial personality, big picture orientation, self-confidence, unwavering dedication and the smarts to hire those who possess the traits to maximize business growth and success. Those we need to hire will oftentimes represent qualities we ourselves do not possess.

The American marketplace abounds with more opportunities than ever. Potential entrepreneurs have a broad spectrum of options to choose from. They can become founders of their own enterprises, start a franchise or distributorship, buy an existing business or create their own brand of products or services. Success on each of these entrepreneurial paths requires a slightly different personality, and matching the personality to the opportunity increases the chances of success.

At this writing, we are several years into our so-called economic recovery. During our official short-term recession most entrepreneurs learned several things: cash is king and cash flow reports become weekly events. We cut as much fat in our organizations as possible and for many of us we've cut into the muscle as well. We've let friends and family go, but we've also survived. As we crawl our way back we will do it with fewer people – the ones who are better. We'll maintain improved banking relationships, providing that's not oxymoronic in its thinking. As we grow, we'll grow cautiously. Because of the uncertain economy, lack of corporate security, economic layoffs, and downsizing, the motivation for people to start their own businesses is greater than ever. Even with the current employment climate, people have greater motivation and sometimes greater flexibility to go into business. As a business owner we rarely get fired; we may fail, but that we can impact. The abundance of possible business ventures makes the dream of owning a business attainable for more people.

Nevertheless, there's a critical shortage of insight into the personality of an entrepreneur. America's television stations, bookstores, radio stations, and newsstands are filled up with "experts" offering basically the same sound-bite information about what entrepreneurship is and how one can succeed as an entrepreneur. The commonly accepted plan for entrepreneurial success works primarily for people who possess an entrepreneurial or leader personality. The experts may profess a singular solution that works best with that singular personality. That's great if you happen to be among the small percentage of the population that has an innate leadership personality. If you don't, the chance that those how-to-succeed-in-business books will work for you is miniscule at best.

I know, I know. If you think I sound too professional, I'm not. I am however self-confident and an expert in this field. I will do my best not to tell you what to do or think, because if you are an entrepreneur then you can't stand being told what to do.

Who IS the Entrepreneur Next Door?

The genesis of this book began when Thomas Stanley and William Danko's book, *The Millionaire Next Door* (Pocket, 1998) was first published. I was one of more than two million readers fascinated with this glimpse into the saving and spending habits of millionaires. Actually, I believe most readers bought it because they wanted to gain insights into how they could also become millionaires. *The Millionaire Next Door* surveyed 400 households with a net worth of $1 million or more. What was interesting to me was that more than 70 percent of the respondents were not entrepreneurs. They were schoolteachers, bus drivers, and professionals such as doctors, attorneys, and CPAs. Only 30 percent of those surveyed were actually entrepreneurs.

It was then that my curiosity got the best of me. I set about comparing Accord Management Systems' survey group with their survey group. The members of our survey group, for the most part, belonged to the Young Entrepreneurs Organization, were under the age of 40 when they completed the survey, and had annual business revenues in excess of $1 million each.

The Next Four Paragraphs are *Really* Important...

Here's the essence of our findings: The Survey group for *The Millionaire Next Door* had an average age of 57 and a net worth of $3.7 million. Our study group had an average age of 31 and a net worth of $3.4 million. How was it that the members of our group were still kids, but had amassed similar net worth in 25 fewer years? They didn't have the advantage of compound interest, but they did have the advantage of possessing very strong entrepreneurial personalities. More important, they were enjoying opportunities that were very well-suited to who they were.

Simply put, measuring one's personality and predicted success for a given role. The world's best bookkeeper has a great bookkeeper personality, a great salesperson has a great salesperson's personality, and a successful entrepreneur has a great entrepreneur's personality. But that doesn't mean a great bookkeeper will become a great financial controller or CFO.

This book has been written with messages specifically designed for people with a range of different personalities. Remember the story about Goldilocks? Some personalities are too big, some are too small, and some are just right. There's no such thing as a good or bad personality. The suitability of someone's personality is more determined by the requirements of the opportunity. Basically, you want to get the right people on the bus and into the right seats. And, you definitely want to be on the right bus and in the right seat yourself!

Some opportunities require a strong bandwidth of personality and some require very little. Each reader has a different personality, and it's typically much different from the author's personality. As an example, if you read a book on leadership by former General Electric chairman, Jack Welsh, and you don't have his strong personality, the stories he shares are good, but they may not help you learn to be a great leader. In this book, however, there are elements, anecdotes and stories that have been written about and for each one of us.

Choice and Destiny

Given my family history, it was surely destined that I would become an entrepreneur. My grandmother, born in the late 1800s, was a sharp businesswoman. Possessing a real estate license and a law degree, grandma was the first entrepreneur in my life. I have fond memories of a two-story house on Main Street that she sold "on contract for deed" at least a dozen times. We called it the yo-yo house. People would make payments for a couple of years and then leave, and she'd sell it again. Each time I was appointed as the official painter and maintenance person. I was also the guy who got something of greater value than the cash. I got the experience.

I also got the education. I graduated with a business degree from Bradley University in Peoria, Illinois. There's an interesting story here. I originally attended Arizona State University from 1969 to 1972 and finished my degree in Peoria, but not in the '70s or the '80s – it was actually the late '90s. I can remember finishing my senior year at Bradley back in 1973. I was three semester hours short of my degree requirements, and Dean Bausch said, "Bill, it's summer school, it's one class, and it will be behind you forever." Like many of you, I have difficulty being told what to do. So it wasn't until almost 30 years later that I went back. I was 48 years young and I was setting my goals. I said that I wanted to have a book written by the time I was 50 and that I wanted to have my college degree. I went back to Peoria and met with the current dean of the School of Business. I petitioned the school to change the residency requirements. I took two classes, passed, and now have my college degree. I also achieved my second goal which was to have a book written by my 50th birthday. And after celebrating that goal, I learned a valuable lesson. There's a huge difference between having a book written and having a book published. Now it has been published, twice.

As much as I appreciate my education and the opportunity to learn new skills, it was clear my personality had the greatest impact on my behavior. Consequently, with the exception of a short three-year sentence with Xerox and Frito-Lay, I've been self-employed for most of my life. I'm a risk-taker, sometimes much to my wife Renee's dismay. We have very different personalities and, while our strengths often complement one another, we tend to approach life from opposite angles. Yet, as co-founders of Accord Management Systems Inc., we're both fascinated with the predictable behavior of entrepreneurs – their strengths and their weaknesses. We refer to weaknesses as "developmental considerations" because it sounds nicer.

This next statement is for the record: I wouldn't be enjoying the same level of success if it weren't for Renee. She's the balance I require in my life. Unfortunately, sometimes I think I benefit more from her than she does from me. Renee has a calming influence on many, whereas I'm more like Captain Chaos or, as she once called me, "Bill the Butthead."

Over the course of 17 years, the employees of my company and I have interviewed and studied the behaviors of more than 20,000 business leaders. We surveyed 1,509 fearless business founders and leaders for this work. Most were under 40 years old, and many were in their 20s and 30s. They had sales of more than $1 million a year. What we discovered from our study is that, different as these entrepreneurs appeared, they shared a number of common personality traits. These traits were the predominant indicators of their success – outweighing education, family ties, skills, and experience.

In fact, of the entrepreneurs we studied, more than 80 percent have very similar personality traits. There's a great deal of truth to the notion that entrepreneurs are born, not made. Although our ultimate behaviors are affected by upbringing, belief systems, education, training, and development, our core personality remains relatively constant throughout our lives. In other words, if you start out as a lion, you're not going to turn into a lamb, regardless of what you do or don't do. There may be times when you can act like a lamb, but it's difficult to maintain that behavior for an extended period of time. For naysayers or those that may be more skeptical ask yourself, "At what age did you notice you were different than the other kids on the block?" It was then that you began to experience the rooting of your personality. In grade school I had a paper route, mowed lawns in the summer, shoveled walks in the winter and sold cookies to go to summer camp. I was different, I just didn't know why.

Some believe our personalities are developed after we're born, as opposed to being something innate. Do you know of a set of identical twins? They may have precisely the same DNA, but their personalities can be very different. There was a recent case in which one of two identical twins was accused of a heinous crime. The authorities had DNA evidence, but couldn't tell which of the twins the culprit was. They looked at more than 100,000 DNA markers and still couldn't tell the difference. Did I mention one of the twins has been in and out of the prison system for most of his life and the other is an upstanding citizen? Go figure.

To experience the greatest level of success and fulfillment, entrepreneurs should choose business ventures that are in-sync with their true personalities. Those who choose well tend to prosper more easily. Those who don't find a fit for their personalities make great material for TV dramas and sitcoms. Can you imagine a receptionist who acts like Rambo or a professional wrestler who acts more like Mr. Rogers? How about a used-car salesman who is quiet and introverted, and doesn't like talking to or interacting with people? You get the idea.

The Entrepreneur Next Door reveals:

- While there are many personality combinations, they can be pretty much divided into seven basic types. Of these, four are entrepreneurial types and three are wantrepreneurial. Synonyms for entrepreneurial may be leader, strategic, big picture, and risk taking. The wantrepreneurs are more tactical experts that prefer risk avoidance and details.
- There are four entrepreneurial generalist personalities and three wantrepreneurial specialist personalities.
- There are critical differences among the seven personality types and how they achieve success in business.
- We *all* have a "Stupid Switch" and we can *all* learn how to turn it off.
- Prospective business areas and opportunities are linked with your personality. These are found at www.theentrepreneurnextdoor.com.
- How the role of self-awareness in the life of an entrepreneur can enhance the entrepreneur's life balance.
- How to create an absolutely awesome business with the right people in the right positions.

The Greatest Knowledge Is Self-Knowledge

Personality is the most important factor dividing entrepreneurs who barely make it from those who make millions. And, more importantly, the awareness of how to harness it, use it, and learn from it. The most successful entrepreneurs know that the greatest knowledge is self-knowledge. They're not necessarily blessed with a higher intellect or more charisma than others, but they understand how to make the best of their talents and how to manage or compensate for their weaknesses. (I usually call weaknesses "developmental considerations" or "potential limitations.")

This book offers an in-depth character study of the seven archetypes that move and shake our world. Our research shows that most entrepreneurs who reach and surpass their goals are natural leaders, strong problem solvers, and work well under pressure. But we've also learned that people who don't have these innate abilities can become very successful if they choose the right business for their personality type and surround themselves with the right people in the right positions. This is a major point.

Through research data, survey results, true stories, and hypothetical scenarios, you will discover how every personality type can grow a lucrative business. The information in this book, coupled with the results of the behavioral assessments provided, will give you priceless insights into your own personality and heighten your self-awareness. You'll find out what makes each of the seven personality types tick and what business might be best suited to your type. The behavioral assessment we used to determine the personalities of our 1,500-plus entrepreneurs was provided by The McQuaig System™ of Toronto, Ontario, Canada. If you want to take the same survey used in the research for this book, then send an e-mail to info@accordmanagementsystems.com and we'll take care of you. Please, only one survey per book.

Are You Taking a Risk?

An entrepreneur was discussing the topic of risk with the host of a radio call-in show. The host said that being in business for oneself was risky. The entrepreneur's definition of risk was living paycheck to paycheck, working for an employer in an "at will" state, where you can be laid off or fired without notice. Or worse, your company could shut down. "That," he said, "is taking a risk."

We discovered that people with natural entrepreneurial personalities have a high level of dominance, are more results-oriented, are independent self-starters, and believe in themselves and their abilities. They don't depend on the opinions of others and often believe that others don't understand them or what they're trying to achieve. People with wantrepreneurial personalities are more accepting, accommodating and agreeable. They tend to be more compliant, want to do things the right way, are more relaxed, and sometimes have higher sociability than those with classic entrepreneurial personalities.

Climbing the Performance Pyramid

The Performance Pyramid (Figure 1.1) represents a cognitive process for determining who you need to be in a particular role or on a particular project in order to achieve the results you seek. Although entrepreneurs can have different personality types, the job behaviors necessary to succeed as an entrepreneur are fairly similar.

FIGURE 1.1: **Five-Tier Performance Pyramid**

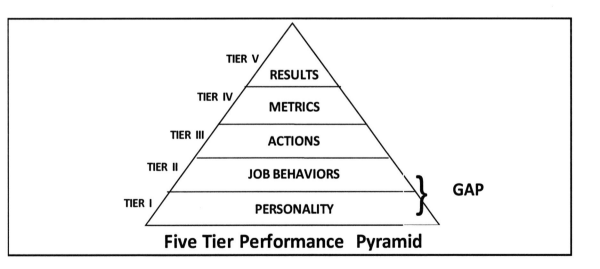

These job behaviors typically require higher than average dominance and above average sociability. To behave in a way that is most beneficial for the business, you might have to override your emotions or natural tendencies, which usually means stretching your comfort zones.

However, if you know that embracing the Actions detailed in Tier III will get the job done, and that you will be rewarded with better results, it will be easier for you to make those actions into a habit, even if they initially feel uncomfortable.

How well you do this is measured by the metrics that you set up for Tier IV and your results are the ultimate outcome in Tier V.

Tier I: Personality

Personality is defined here as a manifestation of a person's core. It is who people are when they are alone. It is the essence of the person who looks back when someone looks into a mirror. Personality is the most stable, least changing aspect of a person's natural style. It develops early in life and remains largely unchanged.

To their benefit, people are able to measure the different aspects of their personalities. I refer to these aspects as factors. It is also possible to measure the level or amount of each of these factors. The bigger these factors are in an individual, the less changeable and pronounced they are also. Conversely, the smaller a factor is, the more flexible it tends to be.

The personality survey/test I used for the research measures four sets of opposing factors located on a continuum. (These factors will be covered in depth in Chapter Four.) See Figure 1.2 for a diagram of these sets of factors.

1. Dominance versus Accepting
2. Sociability versus Analytical
3. Relaxation versus Driving
4. Compliance versus Independence

The two strongest factors in personality are dominance and compliance. When people have more dominance than compliance, they have a more leadership, entrepreneurial personality, characterized by strategic and big picture thinking. I refer to these people as Generalists. When people have more compliance than dominance, they have more of a wantreprenerial personality, which is more tactical, detailed or expert-oriented. I refer to these people as Specialists.

Figure 1.2: **Personality Factors**

High Dominance DOMINANT	High Sociability SOCIABLE	High Relaxation RELAXED	High Compliance COMPLIANT
Low Dominance ACCEPTING	Low Sociability ANALYTICAL	Low Relaxation DRIVING	Low Compliance INDEPENDENT

Source: The McQuaig Institute®. Reprinted with permission

The ability to modify or mitigate people's personalities depends on the strength of each factor and the degree of change they are trying to make. For example, I have learned that it's easier for someone with a dominant personality to behave in an accepting manner than it is for an accepting individual to be more assertive or aggressive. It is also easier for a sociable person to think more analytically than it is for someone who is analytical to be more sociable. It should be noted, however, that sociability is the most malleable or changeable of the four personality factors. People who are driving can appear to be relaxed more easily than relaxed people can be driving. And, it's easier for an independent person to learn to handle details than it is for a compliant person to let go of the details. See Figure 1.3 for the traits that are typically associated with various personality factors.

FIGURE 1.3: **Personality Continuum**

High Dominance	High Sociability	High Relaxation	High Compliance
DOMINANT	**SOCIABLE**	**RELAXED**	**COMPLIANT**
Generalist	Outgoing	Patient	Specialist
Competitive	Friendly	Steady	Conscientious
Goal-oriented	Persuasive	Methodical	Detail-oriented
Risk taker	Collaborative	Loyal	Thorough
Result-oriented	Consensus builder	Prefers a predictable work environment	Prefers a well-defined structure
			Risk adverse
Self-confident	Enjoys interacting with others	Wants to think things through	
		Strong sense of urgency	Strong-minded
Cautious	Work-oriented	Multitasks	Determined
Deliberate	Logical	Works well	Likes freedom
Likes to specialize	Deals with facts	under pressure	of action
Accommodating		Prefers a varied	Strong willed
	Analytical	and active work environment	
Agreeable	Problem solver	Impatient, driving	Independent
Low Dominance	**Low Sociability**	**Low Relaxation**	**Low Compliance**
ACCEPTING	**ANALYTICAL**	**DRIVING**	**INDEPENDENT**

Source: The McQuaig Institute®. Reprinted with permission.

I have discovered and witnessed that if people know and understand the behavioral requirements of a particular position, they have a better chance of manifesting or maintaining those behaviors. It is never easy to do this for an extended period of time, but it is possible. Not surprisingly, people's mindsets often determine how likely they are to fail. Some people believe that no matter what, they can win, whereas others resign themselves to losing before they even begin. Most people are somewhere in between. Regardless of where people are along that range, however, the way they think and how they choose to behave are motivated by their personalities. Thankfully, people also possess the power and the freedom to change their thoughts and actions – at least to some degree.

Research studies indicated that if you have the right personality to do a particular job, your chance for success is five times greater than if you have the wrong personality. There is another side of these studies; that is, there are always those people with the wrong personality for a job, who are still successful.

Tier II: Job Behaviors

The consulting our company has been involved with these past fifteen years has taught us one very important thing: With awareness, a cognitive understanding and the right information, we can take these important steps:

1. Determine the BEHAVIORS required for a task or a position. We actually measure this objectively and behaviorally.
2. Determine and demonstrate the right ACTIONS necessary to accomplish our goals.
3. Determine the correct METRICS to verify our change or growth.
4. When we accomplish these things, we typically achieve our RESULTS.

The process is actually simple and intuitive. For example, an ideal store owner/manager should possess the following qualities:

- Flexibility in moving from one project to another
- Ability to hold others accountable
- Good listener
- Effective communicator
- Convincing

- Independent
- Good with numbers
- Friendly
- Team player
- Visionary

Which of the above qualities are skills (or things you can learn to do or improve upon), and which are determined more by personality? (Trick question by the way – they are all based on personality.) Now, what if people don't have those qualities? Does that mean they can't do the job? NO, NO, NO – It doesn't! What it does mean is that if they can display or adopt these qualities or behaviors, then they will have better alignment with the position's requirements and will ultimately achieve better results. Is it easy? Not necessarily, but it becomes easier when we understand the behavioral requirements of the position.

Tier III: Actions

Actions are influenced by people's personalities and the required job behaviors, or expectations, for a particular role or position. Take a look at the actions that would demonstrate the qualities of a successful store owner or manager in Tier II. Imagine I am discussing the required actions for an owner or manager of a hair salon.

FLEXIBILITY. Multi-tasking – easily moves from one aspect of the business to another, including managing staff and process, interacting with customers, marketing, and selling products or services.

ABILITY TO HOLD OTHERS ACCOUNTABLE. Hires and fires employees, takes corrective action in a timely manner, and confronts people when necessary. Enforces the no day off rule during prom time.

GOOD LISTENER. Lets the speaker express his entire point without interrupting, repeating or paraphrasing. To ensure understanding, writes or records important points so that no details are missed and, most importantly, makes sure the speaker feels he has been heard.

EFFECTIVE COMMUNICATOR. Clearly expresses ideas, giving directions, and describing goals and plans. Says what he means and means what he says, but does so in a way that isn't offensive or defensive.

CONVINCING. Expresses a level of warmth and self-confidence that leads others to believe that his way of thinking is correct and should be followed. This is also akin to collaborating or consensus building.

INDEPENDENT. Operates without strong rules, policies, procedures, or guidelines.

GOOD WITH NUMBERS. Understands and uses the metrics of his business in order to be a better manager or leader. Uses these numbers in a timely way to speed up response time and accountability.

FRIENDLY. Works well with others, asks for their opinions, and values their contributions. Collaborates with and builds consensus with others. Comes out of his office, walks the four corners, and interacts with staff and clients.

VISIONARY. Works on the business, as opposed to in the business. Markets his product, service, or location. Maintains a big picture perspective and works toward long-term goals.

Tier IV: Metrics

Actions (Tier III) without metrics (Tier IV) could be nothing more than misdirected efforts. It is absolutely essential to measure the accomplishments of our actions. Without doing so, how do we know we are progressing or achieving? When you think about it, metrics are everywhere. Even at an early age we had our allowance and considered what we could buy with it or save to buy. Face it – we measure almost everything.

Today's Dow Jones is 13,031. Seventy-one is today's high temperature. The approximate ROI (return on investment) from the purchase of this book will vary. My clients that have 100 employees and sales of $15,000,000 per year have measured a savings of more than $400,000 per year. Assuming the annual cost of our program may be $20,000 per year, their return on investment is 20 times per year.

When a fast food restaurant loses an employee within the first 90 days, their cost of turnover is about $2,500. When a company loses a good sales representative, an engineer, a software programmer, the turnover cost is typically one to one-and-a-half times the employee's annual salary. Remember, unless you measure it you can't manage it.

Tier V: Results

It's interesting to note that personality becomes more important as a person moves up the corporate ladder. Sure, skills are important, but almost every CEO I have worked with has commented that their company's most important asset is having the right people in the right positions. Not every successful CEO has the perfect personality for the job, but the ones who excel understand that certain behaviors and actions are required to generate the results they are seeking.

As you have seen, there is a difference between the behaviors I have listed and the actions that naturally stem from those behaviors. If you were to attach metrics to each action, you could measure the levels of accountability and accomplishment that ultimately provide the desired results. By creating a cognitive approach to succeeding in the role of, say, a franchise owner – people both with and without the preferred personality for this position can accomplish similar results. If you can't measure it, you can't manage it.

A number of authors have espoused the virtues of leadership but, in my opinion, many have missed the mark. They presume that if one leader can accomplish his goals, then all other leaders should be able to duplicate those efforts and therefore get the same results. It doesn't work that way. It works for those with similar personalities and situations. If the author or leader possesses the Tier I capability, understands the Tier II requirements, and has been able to make things a reality because of his Tier III commitments, then it works. Unfortunately, most authors are missing the "how to."

Chapter 1

— The Bottom Line —

➢ Successful entrepreneurs share a number of common personality traits, and these traits are the predominant indicators of their success, outweighing education, family ties, skills, and experience.

➢ The most commonly accepted plan for entrepreneurial success only works for a small percentage of the population, those that have a natural (Tier I) leadership personality.

➢ People who choose business ventures and jobs that are in sync with their true personalities tend to experience the greatest level of success and fulfillment.

➢ Every personality type has the potential to grow a successful business.

➢ The Five-Tier Pyramid (Personality, Job Behaviors, Actions, Metrics, and Results) represents a proven cognitive approach to success.

➢ The ability to modify or mitigate personality depends on the strength of each innate personality factor and the degree of change a person wants to make. We refer to this as Mastering the Gap.

➢ If you have the right personality to do a particular job, your chances of success are five times greater than if you do not.

CHAPTER

2

Your Personality Can Pave the Way to Success

PERSONALITY IS UNDOUBTEDLY THE MOST SIGNIFICANT FACTOR IN understanding why some people can do certain jobs easily while others struggle with the same tasks. Based on my experience and countless interviews, it seems our personalities are pretty much ingrained by the time we are in our late teens. Individuals can, however, have adaptive personalities.

Best-selling books, such as *Good to Great,* by Jim Collins, champion the virtues of "Level Five Leadership" and "getting the right people on the bus." *Now, Discover Your Strengths* by Marcus Buckingham suggests placing employees in positions compatible with their strengths. *Follow This Path* by Curt Coffman may be the first nonacademic book that provides the how-to in managing the developmental side of a business. These books have one common thread: their conclusions are based on substantial objective research.

The missing link in their research is that they measured *organizations,* not the people who founded, managed, or led these organizations. This is critical because they are looking at a level of organizational health or potential dysfunction without considering the strengths of those who create and run these organizations. This is critical because they are looking at a level of organizational health or potential dysfunction without considering the strengths of those who create and run these organizations. It is the leaders of organizations who provide direction and formulate values, mission, and vision. It is the personalities of these leaders and the personalities of their employees that determine how successful an endeavor will be.

The research that my company collected clearly demonstrates how assessing an entrepreneur's core personality is a highly accurate way of predicting his potential, the types of businesses he's likely to enjoy, and the challenges he may experience.

For the past several decades, entrepreneurship has been viewed as a one-size-fits-all process for starting businesses. Only recently have those of us who study this phenomenon concluded that being a successful entrepreneur is about much more. Today, systems of organizational measurement can accurately predict the success or failure of an enterprise based on the personality of the individual who is starting or buying the business. The results of these assessments also indicate in which types of businesses each entrepreneurial personality type is likely to excel. That's significant because it means that everyone, even those who aren't natural-born leaders, can succeed in business ventures by understanding themselves and hiring those with the necessary traits that they themselves may not possess.

I've discovered there's an even greater benefit to knowing and understanding the personalities and tendencies of the people one manages, works for, and/or works with: With increased awareness of others and yourself, you have the knowledge and power to make more intelligent decisions and to choose the most appropriate entrepreneurial path.

The research findings on business success, that my company has amassed, show that four entrepreneurial personality types own and run the majority of successful businesses: Trailblazers, Go-Getters, Managers, and Motivators. A smaller but still impressive number of strong businesses are run by people who possess one of the three

Wantrepreneurial or Specialist personality types: Authorities, Collaborators, and Diplomats. (Chapter Four provides a general description of these personality types.)

The key is for people to be aware of the traits they *do* have and to develop (or hire) the essential success traits they need to bridge the gap.

Why Personality?

The formulation and study of personality from an objective perspective began over 70 years ago. In the early 1930's, Louie Thurstone wrote the book *Vectors of the Mind*, which documented studies finding there was a high level of consistency between a person's choice of descriptive words and his personality. If I felt that terms such as *strong-willed* and *confident* described me, chances were good that I had a more dominant personality.

During World War II, an actuary who worked for the U.S. Army Air Corps was asked to create an assessment that would help the Air Corps determine who would make the best fighter pilots and who would make the best bomber pilots. The behavioral requirements of a bomber pilot include: being careful, precise, matter-of-fact, by-the-book, methodical, calm, introspective, and accommodating. The fighter pilot, on the other hand, is seen as more aggressive, self-confident, outgoing, driving, somewhat casual in his thinking, independent, and strong-willed. The two pilots' personality types are almost opposite. The bomber pilot would look at himself in the mirror before a day's mission and say something to the effect of, "Grant me the ability to drop my payload exactly where it needs to be, allow me the ability to safely return my ship and crew, and above all keep me from screwing up." Meanwhile, his fighter-pilot brethren might say, "Grant me the ability to splash a few of those suckers, and if those bomber pilots don't get out of my way…" Well, you get the picture. This was one of the first real job-fit applications that was determined by assessing the position as well as the applicant.

Entrepreneurs Share Their Favorite Business Mottoes

"We suck less." -Anonymous

"A World that Works Because Business Works." -Frances Fujii

"Find a way." -Shelby Russ

"If it's worth doing, it's worth doing right." -Drew Clancy

"Persist until you succeed." -Doug Evans

"NETWORK exists to make its clients look good." -Linda Tessar

"Have fun and make the kids smile, biz and personal." -Shep Hyken

"With experience comes mistakes, from mistakes comes wisdom. And right makes might."
    -Anonymous

"Bliss in action." -Vince Poscente

"Prosperity through quality." -Wolf Bielas

"Deliver top quality work and have fun doing it." -Ashley Postlewaite

"You cannot do business by remote control." -Karen Caplan

"We are not planning the future, we are inventing it." -Skip Viragh

(Authors note: Skip was the founder of Rydex funds located in Maryland. Skip was a leader extraordinaire. Sadly, he passed away.)

"There's no bigger word in the dictionary than 'if." -Jo-Anne Dressendofer

"Put your head down and get it done!" -Jim Frey

"Poverty sucks!" -Anonymous

"Never give up-'can't' is *not* in the dictionary." -Jay Sweet

Today, personality testing has become a widely used tool to help companies get the people side of their business right. The key to using these tools for selection is measuring the behavioral requirements of the position and comparing them with an applicant's personality. You can't measure an applicant in the abstract; you must measure the applicant against the requirements of a position.

Behavioral studies conducted over the past 30 years affirm that personality can be accurately measured and that this valuable insight-when put to good use- can significantly improve our effectiveness and level of success. It's important to point out that *combinations* of behavioral traits define everyone's personality. Two people who share roughly the same traits aren't carbon copies of each other because their experience, education, and skills must be factored into the formula. With the assessment tools we use at Accord Management Systems, four basic scales measure an individual's natural style of behavior to determine his personality type. Based on these measurements, we compare and contrast an individual's levels of dominance and acceptance; sociability and analytical abilities; relaxation and drive; and compliance and independence. The scientific studies that set us on the path to accurately measuring personality come from the works of Gordon Allport, Louie Thurstone, and other behaviorists.

For the purposes of our behavioral research, we used several proven and reliable assessments. One of the systems we used for personality testing was The McQuaig System™ of Toronto, Ontario, Canada. This 40-year-old system indicates that there are seven personality types that make up a broad spectrum. The personalities that we've termed Trailblazers, Go-Getters, Managers, and Motivators possess the strongest innate entrepreneurial personalities, whereas the Authorities, Collaborators, and Diplomats are the wantrepreneurial personalities. You'll be introduced to each of these personality types, and, as you make your way through the book, you'll gain a greater understanding of what makes them tick and what ticks them off. You'll develop an appreciation for what works for you and for them and what doesn't.

What Determines Success or Failure?

When Did You First Notice You Were Different from the Other Kids?

When I give a presentation, I usually ask the participants, "When did you first notice you were different from others and what were those differences?" In a presentation in New Jersey, one participant had an extremely high level of dominance, a very low level of sociability, was highly driven and was somewhat independent. He was comfortable being by himself. We'll call him Mark.

I refer to Mark's personality type as a Trailblazer. He first noticed he was different from others when he was on the wrestling team in high school. He was under the mistaken impression that wrestling was a team sport. Mark was aggressive and assertive and had a tremendous desire to win. Today as a CEO, he has the exact same motivations. He wants to win all of the time. He knows his employees represent his corporate team, but in the final analysis, Mark feels he is often doing the heavy lifting himself... just the way he likes it.

Looking Beyond the Obvious

Remember when the Human Genome Project was big news? It seemed like almost every day there was another discovery. Once - on my way from Washington, D.C., to a presentation in Minneapolis, I was reading about the Genome Project. As I do with most books, I turned to the index to see whether there was anything written about personality. There was! The authors had surmised that descendants from Scandinavian countries have a tendency to be tall, thin, introverted, and fair in color with both their hair and eyes. I thought, "Cool!" Remember, I was on my way to Minnesota, the home of the Vikings. And the Vikings are from where? My point exactly. The next morning, I prepared for my presentation to the 15 CEOs who belonged to a local CEO peer-to-peer group. My topic was leadership and, in preparation for this workshop, I surveyed the personalities of the 15 members. As they began to arrive, I noticed that almost all of them were tall, thin, blond or bald, and had light-colored eyes and complexion. As I looked at their personality graphs, I found that they were- you guessed it – introverts.

Entrepreneurs Speak Out about Starting a Business

Q: *At what age did you first know you were driven to succeed?*

Eighty percent of this survey group knew they were driven to succeed before they reached the age of 21. Past performance is the greatest predictor of future performance, and these entrepreneurs began their quest at a very early age. They believe in themselves and are willing to be put to the test time and time again.

At what age did you first know that you were driven to succeed?

Age	Percent
11 years old	25%
11 to 15	40%
16 to 20	15%
21 to 25	12%
26 to 30	6%
31 to 35	2%
36 to 45	0%

Chapter 2

— The Bottom Line —

- ➢ Assessing entrepreneurs' core personalities is a highly accurate way to predict their capabilities, the types of businesses they're likely to enjoy, and the challenges they're likely to experience.
- ➢ There's tremendous benefit in knowing and understanding the personalities and tendencies of the people you're managing, working for, and working with.
- ➢ The key to entrepreneurial success is to be aware of the traits you have, and to then develop or hire the essential success traits necessary to bridge the gaps.
- ➢ Behavioral studies conducted over the past 30 years affirm that personality can be accurately measured, and this valuable insight–when put to good use–can significantly improve your effectiveness and level of success.
- ➢ The personalities termed *Trailblazers, Go-Getters, Managers*, and *Motivators* possess the strongest innate entrepreneurial personalities, whereas *Authorities, Collaborators*, and *Diplomats* have wantrepreneurial personalities.
- ➢ Thinking styles and personality are so fundamental that it is easy to overlook their profound influence on teamwork, innovation, market awareness, organizational learning, communication, persuasion, and virtually every other key determinant of business.
- ➢ You can't change your IQ or your personality. You can change your behaviors when you have the cognitive understanding and will.

CHAPTER

3

How the Four Personality Factors Work

IT WAS IMPOSSIBLE TO GET A STRAIGHT ANSWER FROM MY GRANDMOTHER UNTIL AT least my 17th birthday. I can remember asking her, "So, Grandma, how are you feeling?" She would say, "How do you think I should be feeling? I'm 78 years old." Why is this significant? Much of our success is built on the art of the question, and natural-born entrepreneurs have a tendency to ask specific questions, oftentimes determined by their personalities. They have a tremendous natural sense of curiosity. Clearly Socrates had a strong entrepreneurial flair.

The favorite question of the Trailblazers, Managers, and Go-Getters is, "Why?" "Why did you do it that way? Why can't I? Why shouldn't I?" They have a natural curiosity and are always questioning themselves and others. Those who are more compliant, such as the Authorities, Collaborators, and Diplomats, are usually the "How" people. They always want to know how a project or task should be done. They are the true experts and need to do things right because when they do things right, they avoid blame. Those with higher levels of sociability are usually our "Who" people, like Motivators, Collaborators, Go-Getters and Diplomats. They are usually concerned with whom they need to talk to and whom they need to involve, and they are often strong consensus-builders. The "When" people make up one of two types: those who are calm, methodical, as well as those who are more driving, intense, with a high sense of urgency. Having this understanding makes it easier to identify behavioral styles. It also makes it easier to communicate. Remember the "Golden Rule?" It shouldn't be so much 'do unto others the way we want them to do unto us' as much as it should be treating others the way they want to be treated.

The Four Factors

There are four measurable personality factors: dominance, sociability, relaxation, and compliance. Each has two separate or opposite traits. On one side of dominance, for example, people have their competitive side, and the opposite side is accepting or accommodating. Particular combinations of factors produce the seven personality types and behavioral styles.

Dominance

Those with a high level of dominance are competitive and goal-oriented individuals who can be aggressive in resolving uncertainties. Winning is very important to them, and they seek to lead the way in facing new challenges. They aim high and work hard to achieve their aspirations. They face troublesome issues, resistance, and obstacles willingly, and despite them (or maybe because of them), they are determined to attain their goals. They thrive on difficult assignments and tough competition and are usually people of action who make things happen. They tackle problematic situations vigorously, seek to enhance performance and results, and don't want to be controlled. They usually display a wide variety of interests and will seek opportunities to handle many projects simultaneously. Ambitious, needing to succeed, they not only welcome but often expect authority over and responsibility for others. Exceptionally assertive and success-oriented, they show up for one reason: to win.

They are results-driven and goal-oriented, seek the big picture, plan strategically, need opportunities for leadership, and require autonomy, authority, and a degree of power. *Now, check out this interesting tidbit: we have the same personality throughout most of our life. Early in our career we have the same personality, we just aren't in a position to use it. When hiring we need to focus on how we want the person to grow – and then hire for that position.* A high level of dominance is necessary in most sales positions, on the executive team, and in marketing and business development. Dominance is often an essential element for those entrepreneurs who are founders of their endeavors. It's important to note that there are varying degrees of dominance. Sometimes we refer to these people as the "I am right" individuals.

Those with a low level of dominance are more cautious and deliberate, going out of their way to get along with others. They know how to be a part of a team and work for the good of the group rather than seeking out individual recognition. They enjoy working with good people and will take direction from others, as in a franchise environment. They're careful about making decisions and will typically reserve their decisions until they have thoroughly examined all the facts surrounding the case. They consolidate their efforts and specialize in one area or field of endeavor, wanting to concentrate on that area of expertise. Preferring a conflict-free working environment, they often try to mediate quietly, one on one, especially if co-workers are having problems with one another. They are very accepting and cautious; need encouragement, reassurance, and harmony in relationships; seek accord; avoid confrontation; require freedom from competition; are good followers; and prefer to be supportive of others.

Those who have lower levels of dominance are usually more comfortable working in environments where their success is determined mainly by their ability to follow policies and procedures. Examples would be a franchise, a distributorship, and opportunities that have a strong brand or a great location. Within a corporate environment, they do best in most support, manufacturing, customer-service, financial, and administrative positions. They find confrontational and competitive situations difficult.

For extreme examples of dominance levels, think about Rambo and Mr. Rogers. Rambo is the one who is highly dominant, and Mr. Rogers is more accommodating. Which more accurately reflects your Tier I natural style? Are you more of a Rambo or a Mr. Rogers, or perhaps somewhere in between? Approximately 70 percent of our population is a Mr. Rogers type, whereas only 30 percent are more like Rambo.

Sociability

Sociability is a personality factor defined largely by our style of communication. Do you use more words to tell your story, or are you more comfortable using fewer words? Do you have more of a selling style of communication or a telling style? Do you have a preference for working with people, or are you more comfortable working with systems, concepts, and numbers?

People who are highly sociable enjoy receiving recognition, they need more pats on the back, and they want to be part of – or perhaps lead – a well-run team. They need to interact with others and, to seek and build consensus, they want to be part of a respected group. A highly sociable person tends to be outgoing and extroverted, gregarious, stimulating, socially poised, friendly, and talkative. Higher levels of sociability are typically a requirement in positions that involve selling, customer service, and public relations. However, it's important to point out that too much sociability can have the opposite effect; it then becomes difficult to close sales if one has too much sociability, as it can also be difficult holding others accountable. The reason for this is they want to be liked and think if they ask for the order – and the customer says NO – then they've put the relationship at risk. My attitude is, unless someone buys – there is no relationship.

People with lower levels of sociability tend to be more analytical, self-conscious, serious, and introspective. They can even be secretive and remote. Their style of communication can be more matter-of-fact, strictly business, sometimes sparse or perhaps even terse. People with lower sociability need the opportunity to think and analyze and prefer private recognition sometimes based on their expert status.

Those with lower levels of sociability are usually found in the back end of the business – financial, production, research and development, information technology, engineering, and other positions that require less interaction with others. An extreme example of a low sociability job would be a toll-taker where people are by themselves all day. From a leadership or entrepreneurial position, they can be most comfortable working behind the scenes.

A good example of sociability opposites would be Bill Clinton and Bill Gates. Clinton, the more sociable, uses his words to communicate from an empathetic perspective, whereas Gates, the more analytical and introverted, thinks more and talks less. Highly sociable entrepreneurs – a company's chief officer, rainmaker, and chaos creator, for example – can enjoy ventures in which they are constantly meeting and dealing with people, such as in retail, public relations, marketing, and selling. Entrepreneurs with lower levels of sociability might find greater enjoyment in franchising or companies where the customer comes to the store based on advertising, location, or brand awareness. In this environment, the more introverted entrepreneur is excellent at dealing with people because the entrepreneur isn't required to sell. The brand, product, or location does the selling. As an aside, introverts behave like extroverts when they are with those they feel comfortable with, feel safe with and trust. Our population is pretty well equally divided between extroverts and introverts.

Which more accurately reflects your Tier I, natural style? Are you more highly sociable, more analytical, or perhaps a combination of both?

Relaxation

Relaxation, as a personality factor, determines a person's pace of work, sense of urgency, and the speed at which one is comfortable working. Is a person more comfortable dealing with

> **Creatures of Habit**
>
> Those with higher levels of relaxation are often strong creatures of habit. An example would be the highly relaxed technician. Jim travels the country constantly and, given his penchant for regularity, his favorite restaurant is Denny's. He always knows what to expect because each one has very consistent quality, including the same menus. BTW, he always orders the #4.

pressure or would he rather have a more stable, steady work environment?

People with higher levels of relaxation prefer stability and long-term, family-like relationships. They enjoy being rewarded for loyalty, are adaptable to change – with advance notice – and enjoy "familiar" surroundings and activities. A highly relaxed person tends to be more methodical, calm and patient. He does best in jobs that are repetitive in nature. More than 70 percent of our population has a higher than average level of relaxation. Fortunately, more than 80 percent of the jobs in our society require a higher-than-average level of patience because they require the worker to handle repetitive tasks on an ongoing basis. Those with a higher level of relaxation are the backbone of our society. They're the loyal workers who make everything run – and run on time.

People with lower levels of relaxation enjoy freedom from repetition and need a varied pace. They thrive in a changing environment, want fewer controls, and are better at multitasking. A persona with a lower level of relaxation tends to be more intense, driving and sometimes a bit high strung. They work well under pressure and are typically comfortable sharing that pressure with others. They're good in leadership or entrepreneurial roles that are fast-changing and allow for multiple areas of focus.

Think of the fable, *The Tortoise and the Hare*. The tortoise is the more relaxed entrepreneur who does well in businesses that are stable and have predictable levels of pressure. A retail environment is a great fit (except on the days after Thanksgiving and Christmas). Tortoises are the backbone of our society. They work well in operations that offer consistent processes, such as restaurants, where the pace – although hectic – is always predictable. Oil-change facilities, laundries, and photocopy shops are other examples.

The hare is the entrepreneur with a lower level of relaxation (and therefore a higher level of drive) who doesn't find enough challenge in these types of opportunities unless they have multiple locations and are constantly looking at and incorporating ways to improve. It is important to remember who finished the race. One of the challenges that those with *driven* personalities have is they think that everyone should be like them...and that just doesn't work.

Which more accurately reflects your Tier I, natural style? Are you more relaxed like the tortoise, or more driven like the hare? Or, maybe you're a combination of both?

Compliance

In essence, the compliance personality factor is all about the details. Are you good at following procedures and policies, or are you better at working in an environment that's relatively free of structure?

People with higher levels of compliance prefer security, stability, and an understanding of exactly what the rules are. They also deal better with day-to-day responsibilities, tactical applications, strong direction and leadership, opportunities for advanced training, and a job for life. A highly compliant person tends to be precise, cautious, self-disciplined, structured, and sometimes a perfectionist. The more highly compliant entrepreneurs had better be in a business where they're comfortable with rules and structure, which can be found in many successful franchises. They are somewhat risk-adverse. They don't mind taking a risk as long as it is within their area of expertise.

People with a lower level of compliance are more independent and enjoy freedom from structure, freedom from micromanagement, and opportunities to prove their own ideas in a work environment. A less compliant person tends to be more rebellious, unstructured, strong-minded, and sometimes obstinate and self-directed. These more independent people need to do it their own way and will be more comfortable making it up as they go along. Reading a manual is the last thing they want or would be willing to embrace. They don't mind working in environments where they must figure things out for themselves because they deal well with ambiguity.

The original TV show, *The Odd Couple*, provides a good example of compliance extremes. Felix Unger, the professional photographer, is the compliant one. Oscar Madison, the sportswriter, is less compliant and therefore more independent. Oscar figured it out as he went along. This made Felix absolutely nuts. They both got the job done; they just did it differently.

About 70 percent of our population enjoys structure and rules, whereas 30 percent deal well with ambiguity. Which more accurately reflects your Tier I, natural style? Are you more of a Felix who wants structure or an Oscar who wants independence, or perhaps a combination of both? This might be a good time to get reacquainted with the four factors.

Chapter 3

— The Bottom Line —

- ➢ The four primary factors of our personality are dominance, sociability, relaxation, and compliance.
- ➢ Those with a high level of dominance are competitive, goal-oriented people who can be aggressive in resolving uncertainties. Those with lower levels of dominance are more accepting, agreeable, and accommodating.
- ➢ A highly sociable person tends to be outgoing and extroverted, gregarious, stimulating, socially poised, friendly, and talkative. Those who are more introverted are more analytical and reserved.
- ➢ People with higher levels of relaxation prefer stability, enjoy being rewarded for loyalty, are adaptable to change–with advance notice–and tend to be more methodical, calm, and patient. Their more driving opposites are more flexible and work better under pressure.
- ➢ A highly compliant person tends to be precise, cautious, self-disciplined, structured, and sometimes, a perfectionist. Those with lower levels of compliance tend to be more independent. They can also be strong willed as they want to do things their own way.
- ➢ The favorite question of the Trailblazers, Managers, and Co-Getters is, "Why?"
- ➢ Authorities, Collaborators, and Diplomats usually ask, "How?"
- ➢ Motivators, Collaborators, Co-Getters, and Diplomats are looking to involve others, so they often ask, "Who?"
- ➢ Tier I is represented by your natural style of personality. Your success is determined by the relationship between your Tier I personality and your Tier II Job Behaviors. The difference between these two represents a gap. The size of this gap determines the amount of stretching necessary to accomplish the job. The better the fit – the easier it is. The greater the Gap the more energy is required.

CHAPTER

4

Entrepreneurs and Wantrepreneurs

GENERALISTS TEND TO HAVE HIGHER THAN AVERAGE LEVELS OF DOMINANCE and lower than average levels of compliance. For the most part, Specialists are just the opposite, except that Collaborators and Diplomats also tend to have a higher than average level of sociability.

These levels mean that Generalists tend to be natural entrepreneurs. They also mean that Generalists can step on a lot of toes and spend plenty of time in hot water.

Trailblazers

As you can see from Figure 4.1 (Trailblazer Personality Graph), Trailblazers typically have a high level of dominance, are very driven, and have above-average levels of independence and analytical thought processes. Although these Generalists are the type of people who often come to mind when you think about entrepreneurs, Trailblazers' challenge is building and maintaining lucrative businesses. This is because they are more process-oriented than people-oriented. Not to worry – as sociability is the most malleable of the four factors.

FIGURE 4.1: **Trailblazer Personality Graph**

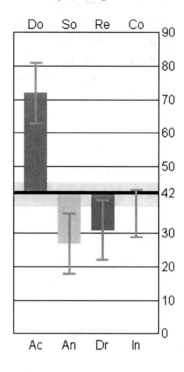

Key to Behavioral Scales

Dominant (Competitive, Goal-Oriented)	< >	Accepting (Deliberate, Cautious)
Sociable (Empathetic, Extroverted)	< >	Analytical (Logical, Work-Oriented)
Relaxed (Patient, Reliable)	< >	Driving (Restless, Pressure-Oriented)
Compliant (Conscientious, Detail-Oriented)	< >	Independent (Strong,-Minded, Persistent)

By nature, Trailblazers are very competitive, ambitious, and goal-oriented – so much that they have a tendency to be aggressive and sometimes take a steamroller approach. Restless and energetic, Trailblazers have a strong drive and display a sense of urgency, regardless of the task at hand. They tend to have two speeds: fast and faster. Independent,

Stupid Switch

The stupid switch is that little part of our reptilian brains that causes us to be more reactive than responsive. It causes us to say NO at the flip of a switch. The default setting is usually in the "on" position.

persistent, and decisive, Trailblazers are logical, analytical, practical, and realistic, and they usually base decisions on facts rather than feelings.

Warning: Do not attempt to sway Trailblazers with an emotional argument, because you won't get what you want. Instead, ask them, "Are you open for a suggestion?" It gives them the opportunity to turn off their stupid switch. That's the little switch located deep within our reptilian brain. It's almost always in the "on" position, but if you ask Trailblazers if they're open to a suggestion and they say "yes," they will listen and be more responsive than reactive, increasing your chances of getting what you want.

Trailblazers are known for stepping on others' toes because of their intense need to achieve their goals and their tendency to focus more on ideas and methods than on people. Although they may be good at routine and details, they often abhor both, seeking challenges and new opportunities instead. They resent close supervision and are likely to be abrasive, so they tend to experience more people problems than other entrepreneurial types.

Go-Getters

Go-Getters have a higher-than-average level of both dominance and sociability and are also very driven and independent. They naturally work by, with, and through others. They are competitive, but their drive to succeed is sometimes tempered by their interest in and concern for others. Ambitious goal-setters by nature, Go-Getters welcome responsibility and authority, but can share some of the spotlight. They are more interested in working with others than in being isolated.

> ### Go-Getters' Creativity
>
> A Go-Getter I recently interviewed said he makes his wife crazy when they attend the Philharmonic. This is because the music stimulates his creativity, so he constantly writes his ideas on a pad of paper that he carries with him.

FIGURE 4.2: **Go-Getter Personality Graph**

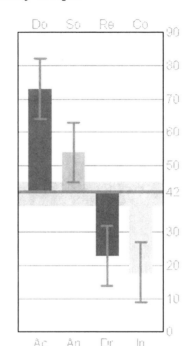

Go-Getters tend to have a high level of energy and often find it difficult to relax. Even when they say they're doing "nothing," chances are they're actually doing *something.* They show a great deal of personal initiative coupled with a compelling sense of urgency to get things done. For Go-Getters, variety really is the spice of life, which is why they quickly become bored and restless with too much routine. They can handle the routine and details when required, but they'd rather not. They relish their independence, work well under pressure, and tend to be persistent and decisive. Go-Getters enjoy motivating others and are usually good at delegating details, but usually not as good at delegating authority. Sociable and outgoing, most Go-Getters are effective communicators, can be very

Defining Clintonesque

Clintonesque: A natural ability akin to that of President William Jefferson Clinton.

During his first presidential campaign, Clinton could walk into a town hall meeting with total strangers and sense their issues. You see this quality in many of the greatest leaders and salespeople. Ronald Reagan also had this quality. In Transactional Analysis, such qualities are referred to as "The Little Professor."

persuasive, genuinely enjoy people, and may even display a Clintonesque quality of empathy and understanding. The Clintonesque Go-Getters are great at reading others.

Go-Getters thrive on challenge and new opportunities and can become surly if they're not achieving their goals. They have distaste for close supervision and balk at most forms of micromanagement. They're more interested in working with others than with ideas, systems, and methods. They're not happy if the work they do isolates them from other people because they need social stimulation.

Managers

Managers are dominant and independent. For Managers specifically, these two characteristics feed off each other – so they can appear to be more dominant or independent than they actually are. Managers are also very goal-oriented and can be quite analytical, focusing more on the process and outcomes than others. These Generalists have a tendency to look at people as vehicles for helping them accomplish their goals. Consequently, they've been known to overlook the people part of the equation, or inadvertently offend people with their straightforward style of communication. Sometimes a bit terse.

Managers have a higher level of relaxation and know that some projects or goals simply take more time to achieve than others. This is unlike the two previous entrepreneurial types, who are also Generalists, but with a greater sense of drive about getting things done quickly. Managers may want something done by tomorrow, but will rarely say they want it done yesterday (a typical comment for Go-Getters, Trailblazers, and Motivators). One of the Managers' strengths is that they like to think things through before responding. They're loyal, sometimes to a fault, as they look at their employees as an extension of their families. And nobody finds it easy to fire family.

FIGURE 4.3: **Manager Personality Graph**

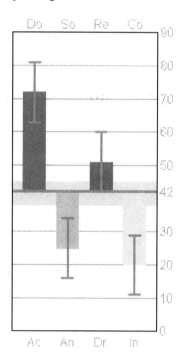

Although Managers have a higher level of relaxation, that doesn't mean they're any less competitive or goal-oriented than their counterparts. They love to win and don't hesitate to take chances. They view conflict, resistance, and roadblocks as par for the course and can often use challenges and difficulties as stepping stones or ways to motivate themselves and others. The problem is that sometimes their strong wills, coupled with their low sociability and high relaxation, can be seen as stubbornness or rudeness.

Managers prosper in environments where they can freely use their sense of initiative and often fight to get their own way—which they firmly believe is the best way or the right way. They make decisions based on facts and are rarely concerned with the opinions or reactions of others. They do not, however, enjoy working with difficult people and will attempt to sidestep personnel problems or steamroll these people, rather than find a way to work things out.

Because Managers are so reliable and patient, they work well with systems and methods and might be described as calm, cool, and collected—even when the pressure is intense and the stakes are high.

Motivators

Motivators, who also fit the Generalist pattern, have a high level of sociability, an above-average level of dominance, and low levels of compliance and relaxation – meaning they are independent and driven. See Figure 4.4.

Typically friendly and outgoing, Motivators do their best work when interacting with others. They're congenial, optimistic, and focus more on the positive aspects of business than on the negative. They believe in others and are supportive and encouraging. Motivators are enthusiastic about sharing their ideas. They work well within a team environment and often enjoy healthy competition with others. A team win is more important to them than a personal win.

> ### The *Can-Do* Motivator
>
> My writing mentor and coach, Toni Robino, is a Motivator. The name of her firm is *With Flying Colours*. Motivators are one of the best personalities to work with because they are always upbeat and positive, and have that marvelous can-do attitude. She works phenomenally well under pressure and makes last-minute deadlines look like an art form.

Motivators are independent, think autonomously, and are capable of acting on their own. They tend to believe their ideas are right and are often determined to get their own way, but will do so by working with and through others. They're persistent, have a strong ability to follow through, and stay on track to get their desired results. Although they don't have to be in charge, they prefer leadership roles and enjoy using their initiative. Motivators tend to be restless, so they want to get things done quickly. They set goals that they think are attainable and don't involve too much unnecessary risk.

Motivators prefer to avoid friction with others, but they'll face up to a problem if and when it can't be avoided. Even so, their high level of sociability can lead them to steer clear of confrontation in an effort to be well-liked and popular with others. They're usually good communicators, but not always as good at listening as they are at talking. They aren't happy in situations that require solitude for long periods of time and, although they can take charge on occasion, Motivators don't respond well to having authority over others in difficult or confrontational situations. They would be better served having the sales manager report to them rather than the whole sales team.

FIGURE 4.4: **Motivator Personality Graph**

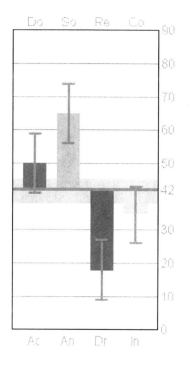

Although Authorities, Collaborators, and Diplomats do not have the most innate entrepreneurial traits, success comes with the desire and the will to learn.

The achievements and failures of Specialists in the entrepreneurial arena are typically determined by how well they can expand their comfort zones and increase their skill sets. We refer to this as their ability to Master their Gaps.

Authorities

Authorities are the backbone of our society. They are the loyal workers who make our world work. They're the ones who make our products, service our systems, and always do it right. They are rarely the founders of entrepreneurial enterprises, but these Specialists can be excellent distributors or franchisees. Also, they can do very well when they purchase an ongoing operation.

FIGURE 4.5: **Authority Personality Graph**

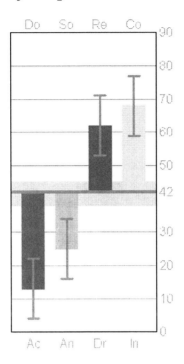

Authorities are detail and tactically oriented and are motivated by doing things one way: the right way. They are very conscientious and cooperative, and follow rules, procedures, and policies carefully. Very thorough with details, they're cautious, deliberate, logical, and analytical, and they make decisions based on facts and figures, rather than on emotions or gut reactions. Relaxed, patient, and peaceful by nature, Authorities are great team players and tend to avoid confrontation.

Steady and reliable, Authorities are comfortable with and can enjoy routine. They aren't necessarily competitive, strong-willed, or highly independent and probably won't want responsibility for difficult people or for difficult decisions outside their areas of expertise. Within their areas of expertise, however, they make quick decisions and can appear to be as strong as most Generalists; their strength just comes from another source—their experience and skills. Their relaxed and easygoing nature isn't usually compatible with pressure and deadlines. That's not to say they can't deal with pressure; as with any pattern or behavior that requires change, they just need an understanding of the actions necessary. Whereas Generalists are the "I am right" people, Specialists are the "It is right" people.

Once the Authority understands the how-to, then they need to take those actions and get the energy to accomplish their goals. At times I refer to their personalities as falling into the drill sergeant pattern, because they're relatively non-confrontational as long as others are doing things right. However, they can become confrontational when others fail to follow the rules.

Collaborators

Collaborators have a Specialist, or expert personality. The primary difference between them and Authorities is that Collaborators have a personality gift called sociability. It is this characteristic that allows Specialists to use their influence to get what they want.

They're good at working in customer-service roles, retail sales, or any environment where being convincing is an important aspect of getting the job done right. There is a difference between selling cold and having a warm market. Generalist personalities are typically better selling in a cold market, whereas Collaborators can be great salespeople because they use their sociability to sell their expertise.

Collaborators work well within a society of rules, politics, and procedures because they are typically thoughtful, considerate and easy going. Great as a part of a team, they're sociable and outgoing, understand people, and like being helpful. Being conscientious and cooperative, Collaborators follow company rules and directions well. Having a higher-than-average level of patience, they like to think things through before responding, especially new situations or new information. They're good at handling details and will produce high-quality work.

From an entrepreneurial perspective, the Collaborators work well within structured environments where a people element is part of the formula for success. They're good at delegating authority, as long as they can hire people who will be loyal and follow the rules.

Collaborators aren't necessarily confrontational or even overly strong-willed (independent). Usually they won't want responsibility for supervising others or making difficult decisions outside their areas of specialization. If they find themselves in that situation, however, they can still get the job done because of their high level of compliance. They can be rather forceful as long as they know what they're talking about. Take Collaborators to areas outside their expertise and they'll want to become experts in those areas before they're comfortable with those decisions. They run the risk of wanting to be liked at the expense of getting results, which is why they're more comfortable working with people than with systems. Provided they're supported in the organization by a "hit man" –

someone to do their bidding and hold others accountable – they can reach their entrepreneurial desires.

FIGURE 4.6: **Collaborator Personality Graph**

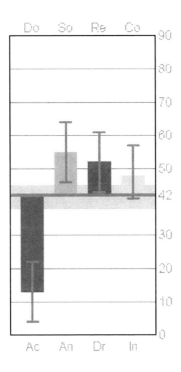

Diplomats

Diplomats are restless and driving people who enjoy working with a certain degree of pressure. These Specialists get things done quickly and work well with deadlines. They find that artificial deadlines can serve them well. They're adjustable to change and deal well with new situations. They have a high sense of urgency, they like variety, and because of their compliance and need to do things right, they work at their full capacity. Diplomats multitask and keep a variety of jobs going at once. Active and energetic, they vigorously attack the parts of their jobs that they enjoy.

Diplomats are conscientious, sincere, and serious when it comes to their jobs. Good planners, who like to prepare for contingencies, follow directions carefully and are thorough with details. They are good team members and can also lead in certain situations. They have a need to become true authorities within their areas of expertise. They can experience difficulty in delegating details, but do a great job when they can do the work themselves.

Diplomats are sociable and outgoing. They genuinely like people and enjoy working with and through others. Empathetic and possessing a chameleon-like quality, they're excellent in most customer-service environments. They're able to see different points of view and they allow others to speak their minds. In general, they get along well with others. They're also optimistic and tend to see the positive side of things.

As leaders, Diplomats are naturals at working with teams and building consensus in dealings with others. A careful approach to decision-making is their natural style.

They avoid taking needless risks and use their natural consensus capability as the linchpin of their decision making. They will almost always examine all available options before moving forward.

FIGURE 4.7: **Diplomat Personality Graph**

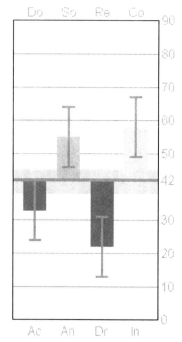

Personality Factors and Entrepreneurship

According to our research, personality basically comes in three broad classifications. First there are the Generalists, who have much greater dominance than compliance and tend to be more strategic and big picture in their thinking. They're also more results-oriented when working in a structure-free environment.

The second classification is the Specialist. I also refer to these as the Wantrepreneurs. The Wantrepreneurs have higher levels of compliance than dominance, which means they are more risk adverse, as opposed to Generalists who are willing to take risks. The Specialists prefer doing things within a structure, one way, the right way. They are more tactically oriented and focus more on the details.

The third classification, a relatively small percentage, was neither Generalists nor Specialists. These were individuals who had almost the same amount of dominance as compliance and therefore we refer to them as those in transition for a relatively short period of time. When these people are surveyed again six months to a year later, their results usually put them in either a Generalist or a Specialist classification.

Success or failure is usually due to personal characteristics, such as attitude, motivation, and temperament (personality), according to industrial psychologist Jack H. McQuaig, founder of the McQuaig Institute®. To measure these key personal characteristics, 50+ years ago McQuaig developed the assessments that comprise The McQuaig System™ today. Using the McQuaig Institute's Word Survey on more than 1500 men and women (all members of the Young Entrepreneur's Organization), Accord Management System's survey of the personalities of the entrepreneur, the generalist, emerged.

Hackett & Associates (HRC Inc.) completed its analysis as a part of this study of 1509 YEO members (1,270 males and 239 females). (See Figure 4.8) Entrepreneurs (Generalists) represented 78.7 percent of the group, 12.3 percent were Wantrepreneurs, (Specialists), and 9 percent were in transition. The predominance of the entrepreneurial personality among YEO members is evident among both males (80.2 percent) and females (70.7 percent).

The mean scores show the levels of the four factors out of the 168 possible points, which makes a score of 42 an average score. For example, if someone scores a 56 dominance, he has a higher than average level of dominance.

The men and women in the study have very similar personalities. They are both Generalists. Both have more dominance than any other factor, and both have dominance that is greater than their sociability, although the men have a bigger spread between dominance and sociability. Both the men and the women are very dynamic and both are relatively independent.

FIGURE 4.8: **Male & Female Entrepreneurs Are More Alike**

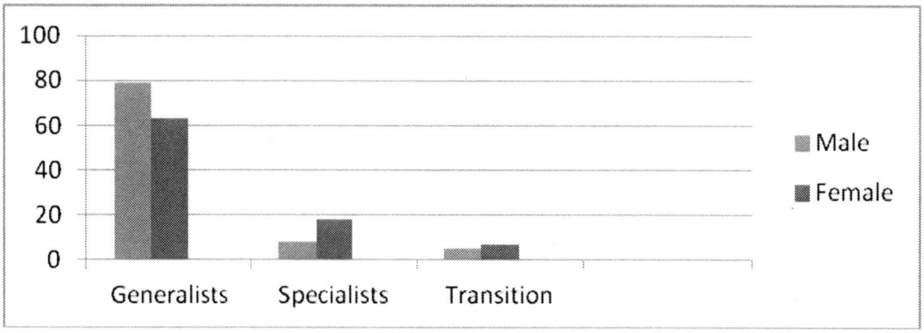

Distribution of Word Survey Profiles

The men have a low of 28.5 to a high of 64.1, so they have a 35.6 point spread. The women, on the other hand, range between 25.3 and 56.3, and a 31 point spread. So the men actually have a slightly bigger personality. What that means is that the male personality will have a greater ability to have an impact on an environment that may be slightly larger, but with the difference of only 4.6 points, it's not statistically significant. What becomes more significant is the edge that the men may have because their dominance is so much higher than their sociability. That also means the men will have the ability to anger more people more often.

The differences are that male respondents had a greater level of dominance and a 20-point spread, or difference, between their sociability and their dominance. Because of this spread, men have a pronounced edge (not necessarily a good thing), a telling style of communication where they actually take on some of the Trailblazer qualities. They also tend to have a more technical orientation looking at life via systems, concepts, ideas, techniques, and technologies.

Scores for the entire group show a profile described as highest in dominance, next highest in sociability with substantially lower levels of relaxation and compliance. This profile of high dominance and sociability and low relaxation and compliance typify an entrepreneurial personality profile that is often seen in founders of new ventures. It is also of interest that women scored high on both dominance and sociability, whereas men scored substantially higher on dominance than they did on sociability. Based on these scores, specifically the higher level of sociability, it can be said that female entrepreneurs will be better than their male counterparts at delegating authority and building consensus, relationships, and teams.

FIGURE 4.9: **Female vs. Male Entrepreneur Graphs**

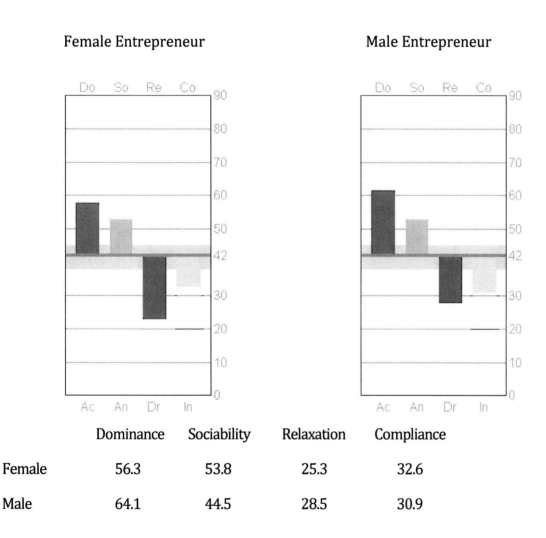

	Dominance	Sociability	Relaxation	Compliance
Female	56.3	53.8	25.3	32.6
Male	64.1	44.5	28.5	30.9

The total spread between the males' lowest factor (drive), and their highest factor (dominance), is 36 points. (For women, the spread is 31points.) As you can see in Figure

4.10, the further from the norm line (42 points) the stronger the personality. The closer the norm line is, the more flexible or malleable the personality.

FIGURE 4.10: **Deviation in the McQuaig System™**

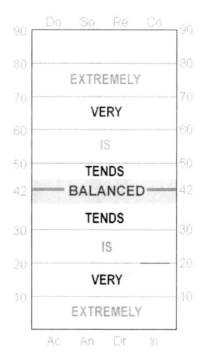

The spread takes on great meaning when you consider that 68 percent of the population has a personality with about a 20-point spread between 30 and 50. Those with a factor greater than 70 or less than 10 represents only three percent of the population. This is basically a bell curve.

Note: *The more a trait deviates from the 42 line, the stronger the behavior will appear to be.*

The size of one's personality determines the size of the environment or organization that one can impact. Bigger is not always better. Due to the relationship between the drive and compliance, the study group would be able to focus on and control the details of the operation, and at the same time be independent enough in the order to deal with ambiguity. Because of the relationship that exists between the very high dominance and the much lower sociability, those individuals with the most extreme spread would display a very controlling side.

In its purest form, however, the Go-Getter personality represents 31.1 percent of the study group. In order for there to be such a high spread between the dominance and the sociability in the

YEO mean scores, look no further than the pie chart that shows Trailblazers represent 28.9 percent of the study group.

FIGURE 4.11: **YEO Chart of Personality Types (N=1,509)**

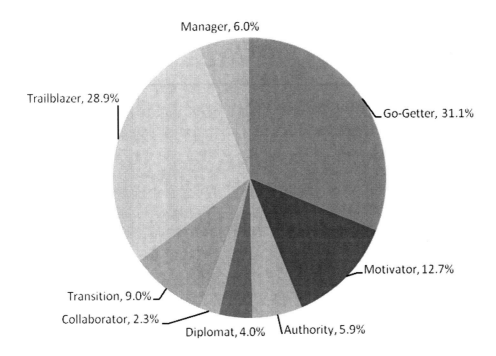

As you may well know, motivation is short-lived. I know this flies in the face of many motivational speakers' messages, but we can rarely maintain changes for more than 30 days based on emotional buy-in.

I created the Five-Tier Performance Pyramid (Chapter 1, Figure 1.1) so the entrepreneurs I coach could have a concrete, cognitive model and process, one they could rely on whether they're feeling motivated or not.

We each predominantly fit one of the seven types listed initially in this chapter. Your personality type represents Tier I on the Performance Pyramid. If you are a Generalist, specifically a Go-Getter or Trailblazer, then it will feel more natural for you to enact the necessary job behaviors to become a successful entrepreneur. If you are not a Trailblazer or a Go-Getter personality then it is essential to look at Tier I in relationship to the requirements of the position, Tier II. The difference between these creates a behavioral gap and it is that gap that needs to be managed.

It is here that the model really began to develop as I realized there were specific actions (Tier III) that support the Tier II requirements. Examples of these actions for a shop owner might include visiting with the local chamber of commerce, joining a networking group (e.g. Business Network International), creating a local neighborhood marketing plan that includes mail, welcome wagon, advertising or personal visits, and determining a way to measure these actions (Tier IV). If the shop owner is able to reach the acceptable Tier IV (Metrics), then I can almost guarantee he or she will reach the desired Tier V (Results).

My associates and I have tested this model thousands of times and, based on our research, it works and works well. If an entrepreneur can accept the changes necessary from a cognitive perspective he can also reach his goals.

Because Trailblazers have a high level of dominance and a lower level of sociability, there is a tendency for the spread to be great in the overall comparisons. Women within this study group have more sociability and more drive than the men. This allows them to work at a faster pace, put more pressure on themselves and others, multitask at a greater level, and use their sociability to get what they want. They can manage others more effectively, handle relationships more smoothly and naturally, build consensus and collaborate with others. The women's pattern has a spread of 31 points between highest and lowest personality factors (only 5 points less than their male counterparts) because the really significant sex difference is the spread between dominance and sociability. The women's differential is only 3 points compared to the men's 20 points. The men's differential allows their dominance to literally take over their personalities.

The bottom line is all about job-fit. If you have a personality (Tier I) that matches the behavioral requirements of the position (Tier II), then the chances of doing well in that position go up exponentially. And, if you don't have the right personality....well, you will just have to work harder. But why not find an opportunity that fits just right? For more on finding the right fit, see Chapter 13: The Goldilocks Theory.

Chapter 4

— The Bottom Line —

- ➤ Personalities can be objectively measured.
- ➤ There are three broad categories of personalities. They are Generalist, Specialist and Transition personalities.
- ➤ Generalist personalities have a strong tendency to be strategic thinkers, big picture, preferring to be measured by overall results, more risk-oriented. Within this there are four types of Generalists consisting of Trailblazers, Go-Getters, Managers, and Motivators.
- ➤ Specialist personalities are more tactical thinkers, detail-oriented, experts, more risk adverse. There are three types of Specialists: Authorities, Collaborators, and Diplomats.
- ➤ Transition personalities have a similar amount of both dominance and compliance, thereby making it difficult to really determine the personality.
- ➤ The Stupid Switch is that little part of our reptilian brain that causes us to be more reactive.
- ➤ Female entrepreneurs seem to have more drive and sociability than their male counterparts.
- ➤ Male entrepreneurs seem to be more aggressive and analytical than their female counterparts.

CHAPTER

5

The DNA of Entrepreneurial Success

EVERYONE IS GOOD AT SOMETHING. RARELY IS ANYONE GOOD AT EVERYTHING. And like it or not, very few people achieve real success in ventures that aren't good fits with their innate personalities. So if you want to start a company, get a job, or invest in an opportunity, doesn't it make sense to learn more about the person you are and what makes you tick? If you're going to be hiring and managing people, wouldn't it be a good idea to know who they really are and how they compare to the behavioral requirements of the position?

The Benefits of Understanding Personality

Understanding your personality and the personalities on your team gives you an incredible edge. If you're a believer in the golden rule, "Do unto others as you would have them do unto you," it's time to reconsider. Although the adage sounds good, it will please only the people who are just like you. Instead, consider doing unto others as *they* want you to do unto them. In other words, treat others as they want to be treated.

Warning: Don't assume you know how someone wants to be treated.

Secret: Knowing someone's personality gives you accurate insight as to what type of treatment will trigger the response both of you desire.

Even without knowing someone's personality profile, you can make a fairly educated guess at his personality type by paying close attention to what he says, what he does, and how he does it. For example, is he a risk-taker or a risk-avoider? Does he seem to enjoy working with people or systems? Does he seem to multitask, or does he prefer to finish a project before starting another?

Imagine that you walk into a conference room for a committee meeting with a handful of people you've never met. All of you have volunteered to be a part of the committee, so you can assume that you either have some level of sociability or a need to achieve or control. Otherwise, the typical tendency would be to avoid (or at least *not* volunteer for) group or team situations.

The first objective is to select a committee chairman. Before the introductions have begun, Sally says, "Let's get down to business. We don't have much time and I have a lot of experience in this area, so I'd like to get things started and make myself available to serve as the interim committee chair."

George interjects, "Maybe it would make the most sense to review the objectives for our committee and then take a vote."

Karen agrees with George: "We probably all have experience in this area so, to keep the process fair, I think we should get to know each other a little and then consider our options. But I'm open to whatever the rest of you are thinking."

Tom says, "Voting sounds good to me." With a soft chuckle he adds "Just don't put my name in the hat. But if you need me, I'd be willing to help out." Everyone but Sally laughs.

Karen turns to Stuart, who has been quiet up to this point, and asks, "What do you think?"

Stuart has the look of a deer in headlights. He swallows and says, "I'm here for your computer support. It doesn't matter to me who is in charge, as long as it's not me."

Of the profiles you read in the previous section, which one do you think fits each committee member? Take a moment to consider the possibilities before you read further.

Sally exhibits high dominance by suggesting that she be in charge. It shows she's more analytical (less sociable) by expressing more interest in the objectives than meeting the rest of the people on the committee. She doesn't laugh when Tom introduces a little humor to the mix. Sally is probably a Trailblazer.

> ## Humor
>
> **Those** with higher levels of dominance and lower levels of sociability have a strong tendency toward sarcasm. Throw a little drive into the mix, and you get a quick wit. Think about Jim Carrey, Robin Williams, Ellen Degeneris, and David Letterman. They are all introverts who often prefer to be by themselves.

(This doesn't mean Trailblazers don't have a sense of humor, but "fun" tends to take a back seat to results when they're on a mission.) George is willing to disagree with Sally's suggestion and puts forth his own idea by suggesting a vote. The willingness to challenge Sally shows that he also has high dominance; but his desire for group consensus indicates that he has a higher level of sociability than Sally. George is most likely a Go-Getter, but possibly a Manager.

Karen attempts to increase the comfort level in the meeting, showing a higher degree of cooperation and acceptance. She supports George's idea to vote, but also says she'll go along with whatever the others want. She doesn't want to be part of a conflict, which is on a par with her cooperative and accepting nature. She suggests that the members get to know one another a little, which indicates that she's sociable – but also willing to express her own ideas. She also asks Stuart to share his thoughts, again showing her tendency to be cooperative or build consensus. Karen is probably a Diplomat.

Tom makes it clear he doesn't want to be the one in charge but suggests that he's willing to assist. This indicated his above-average dominance, though not nearly as above-average as Sally and George. He has an easy way about him and makes a joke, indicating high sociability. Tom seems to be a Motivator or possibly a Diplomat.

Stuart, who doesn't say a word until he's specifically asked to comment, shows a more accepting and analytical side. His statement that he doesn't want to be in charge indicated his accepting nature, and asserting his specific role as "computer support" indicated he wants to stay in that role. Stuart is most likely a Specialist/Authority.

Short-Term Personality Changes

With all that said, keep in mind that people can exhibit behaviors that are significantly different from their natural personalities, at least for short periods of time. Introverts can behave like extroverts, especially when they're with a group of introverts that they trust and feel comfortable with. When someone they don't know walks into their environment, they may return to their more introverted roots. We all have the ability to stretch or hold back our natural styles for a relatively short period of time. The challenge is changing our personality for an extended period.

Just think back to your last job interview, and compare your behavior with the way you acted the last time you went out with one of your good friends. Notice any differences? Anyone who has ever interviewed for a job knows that his "interview personality" isn't necessarily his real personality. Interviewing and dating are basically "sales calls." In both of those scenarios-when we're interested in the job or our date-we're selling ourselves. Our objective is for the person conducting the interview to offer us the job or for the person sitting across from us at a candlelit restaurant to be interested in a second date.

For the most part, personalities, Tier I, developed largely during the early formative years of people's lives, change little over the course of their lives. However, their behaviors, Tier II, are the manifestations of their personalities. They are also the changeable aspects of their personalities. People can change their behavior to get what they want in a number of environments. I like to use the typical dating personality or vacation personality to illustrate your ability to behave outside your natural personality because almost everyone can relate to it. Regardless of your personality, the dating personality you exhibit, (particularly on the first few dates), is probably quite different from what your parents and best friends see.

Imagine you're on a date; perhaps it's the beginning of a relationship. Do you think that you'll be more aggressive or more accepting? The dating personality is usually accepting. "You're 35, and you live with your mother. That's great. What a wonderful way to show your love and support for her!" When you're on a date, do you think you'll be more calm and patient or more anxious and impatient? The survey says you'll be more patient. Imagine it's time to pick up your date. You expect your date to be ready by 6:30. You have plans to see a movie at 7:00, but your date isn't ready. Do you blow a gasket or do you say, "That's ok. Why don't we just have dinner first and then play the rest of the evening by ear?" Right! You're more patient. For those of you currently married, are you still as patient? I doubt it.

When dating, do you find that you're more sociable and outgoing, or more shy and introspective in your thoughts? Most of us are more sociable. For those of us who think selling is just like lying, even we can increase your sociability in the dating process.

FIGURE 5.1: **Dating or Vacation Personality**

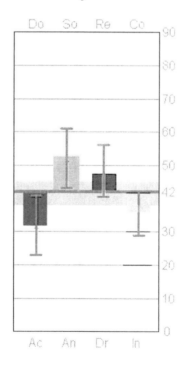

Changing Personalities is a Transitory Occurrence

My wife Renee and I took our three children, Josh, Rebecca, and Alex, to Hawaii. It was definitely a honeymoon-like environment (except for the kids). One day, Josh and I were lounging by the pool when he asked me if he could get a smoothie. Do you have any idea how much smoothies cost in Hawaii? They are $8. (They justify the price by saying they have to import the fruit from the mainland.) I said, "Sure, just charge it to the room." (I wanted to make sure I got both my miles and points.) Several minutes later Josh returns with his smoothie, but also with a grimace. I said, "What's wrong?" He said, "It tastes more like mom's coffee, not like chocolate. Dad, why don't you take this one and I'll get another?" What would you do? It's the family vacation ... so we went back to the smoothie stand and traded it in for a new smoothie. For two weeks I was being the perfect vacation Dad. (That is Tier II behaviors for wonderful, accommodating, and agreeable.) Can any of you relate to this story? To make a long story short, we were at the airport coming home and my wife, Renee, stops me – puts her palm on my chest and asks, "Who's getting on the plane with me? Is it the Bill I have grown to love all over again on this trip, or is it Bill the Butthead?" I responded, "Who would you like it to be?" Renee said, "If it is Bill the Butthead, perhaps you should think about staying here in Hawaii." We can change our personalities for short periods of time.

Do you feel more relaxed or driving when dating? Are you more compliant, trying to do everything right, or more casual and independent? When dating, we have a tendency to be more relaxed and independent in that we're more flexible and uninhibited. This is a great personality to have in a dating environment.

The dating personality is very resilient, quite able to sustain itself for the entire dating process. The challenge with the dating personality is that you're able to be this person for a couple years, but then one morning you awake, look at your significant other and say, "I can't believe how much you've changed since we got married." With shock, they look at us and say, "I'm not the one who has changed. You're the one who has changed." The truth is, both of you have changed because everyone changes.

While dating, interviewing, or in a selling or speaking role, you can project a personality that's completely different from your everyday nature. The bigger the difference between the way you're acting and your natural style, however, the harder and more stressful it will be to keep up the act. (Those of you who are attempting this know exactly what I mean!) Eventually, for most people, the mask falls off. If you meet someone who appears to be calm, cool, and collected, all you have to do is put him in a stressful situation to unveil the person behind the mask. The best novelists learn to do this with the characters in their stories to give readers the inside scoop on the character's true nature, showing their strengths and weaknesses.

Find the Long-Term Personality

According to the Talmud, an important book in Judaism, before a woman shall marry a man, she should see him under three conditions. True personality traits tend to come out when someone is drunk, sick, or angry. I jokingly tell executives who are hiring, "If you really want to know what someone's like, take them out for bad sushi, offer them a couple of martinis and then piss them off and see what happens."

Of course, it would be easier and less painful to have them take a personality assessment. A good example would be Mel Gibson. Remember a number of years ago when he was busted in Malibu for drunk driving? He unloaded on the officer with a string of nasty comments. The next morning when he awoke, he said he wasn't really himself the previous night. Truth be told, he was being himself exactly. Usually, however, he's sober enough to maintain his cool. Enough said...

Since founding and running a successful company is a long-term process, it's best for an entrepreneur to carefully choose a venture well suited for his natural personality. The bottom line is that each of the seven personalities is more compatible with certain businesses than it is with others. Rather than swimming upstream with the currents running against your potential success, why not focus on the types of situations and businesses in which you can thrive?

The value of understanding your own personality is that you can leverage your strengths, improve your weaknesses/limitations, and discover the type of organization you're best served to create. You have two choices; you can either choose a business that is perfect for you, or know you will need to surround yourself with the right people.

Chapter 5

— The Bottom Line —

- ➤ You can make an educated guess on someone's personality type by paying close attention to what they say and do and the way they say it and do it. But remember, it is only a guess.
- ➤ People can exhibit behaviors that are significantly different from their natural personalities, at least for short periods of time. Examples would be dating, vacationing, and interviewing. If you can't tell who you are marrying after five years of dating, then how can you tell who you are hiring after a 30-minute interview? The truth is you can't tell who someone really is.
- ➤ Personalities [Tier I] change very little over the course of one's life. Behaviors (Tier II), however, are changeable. A key to performance is developing an understanding of the Actions (Tier III) necessary to accomplish our goals.
- ➤ Without Tier IV Metrics there is no way of knowing if our actions accomplish our goals. When our Tier IV Metrics supports our Tier III Actions we achieve our Tier V Results.
- ➤ The bigger the difference between how you're acting and your natural style, the harder and more stressful it will be to keep up the act.
- ➤ True personality traits are difficult to mask, especially when someone is drunk, sick, or angry.
- ➤ By understanding your personality, you can leverage your strengths, improve your weaknesses and limitations, and discover the type of organization that you're best served to create.

CHAPTER

6

Behavioral Bottlenecks

SEVERAL YEARS AGO I READ "THE GOAL" BY ELIAYU GOLDRATT. IT WAS ALL about constraint theory. One of the examples used was the question raised about a Boy Scout troop that was on a 10-mile hike. The challenge is that the 12 Scouts are hiking on a rather dangerous trail and must stay fairly close together. Their goal is to leave together and arrive together. They are walking at an average pace of 2.5 miles per hour. The question is... how long will it take to complete the hike? Traditional problem solving might say it will take four hours to cover the 10 miles. The challenge is that the troop doesn't walk at the average pace; they walk at the pace of the slowest scout.

In business we can see our bottlenecks. A forklift breaks and we fix it. A computer crashes and we call IT, but what happens when a person fails to get the job done? People can become bottlenecks the same as faulty equipment. The difference is that behavioral bottlenecks are more difficult to recognize.

At the end of this chapter you will find two blank forms for your homework. These are your Personal Action Plan forms to determine your strengths and your developmental areas. Those listed in this chapter only represent about 10 percent of those created by The McQuaig Institute®. These are for your private use only. Should you desire additional information about The McQuaig System™ or other assessments, go to:

www.accordmanagementsystems.com.

> **Quintessential Trailblazer**
>
> Dwight Sandlin, the senior partner and founder of Signature Homes in Pelham, Alabama, has a Trailblazer personality. Dwight hates to be sold but he loves to buy. As a leading homebuilder in the Birmingham area, Dwight was approached by the ABC television show Extreme Makeover: Home Edition. On "Bullhorn" Day, Monday, January 31, 2005, Dwight and hundreds of his employees and subcontractors pitched in and built a home for the Harris family. This was enough for the Harris family, but it wasn't enough for Dwight. He went to work on his Rolodex and was successful in finding people willing to guarantee college experiences for Chris and Diamond Harris' children.

Perhaps the greatest form of knowledge is self-knowledge. Highly successful people are not necessarily blessed with a higher intellect or more charisma than others, but they typically know how to make the best use of their talents. They also know how to avoid pitfalls that could limit their success. They are either naturally gifted in understanding themselves, have learned from their mistakes, and/or have had great mentors who coached and guided them.

This chapter will help you identify your strengths and teach you to become aware of your weaknesses. If you're married, the weakness side has already been shared with you. (This is a bit of humor. Not much.) These potential limitations decrease your effectiveness. This knowledge will enable you to improve your performance, increase your job satisfaction, and achieve greater success.

The challenge in writing about great companies or their leaders is what if they are only great for a snapshot and not for the full-run motion picture? We see this all too often, especially when it comes to the fastest growing companies. How many of the high tech companies of the 1990s are still around today? Very few. A number of years ago, *Inc.* magazine wrote a cover story about a young entrepreneur that they labeled the next Bill Gates. I believe that Bill Gates has either a Trailblazer or a Manager personality. This cover story was about a hyper-growth entrepreneur with a Motivator personality. He was one of the greatest salespeople I've ever met. The challenge with that high level of sociability is that they have difficulty holding others accountable and typically are not the most analytical. He struggled with this Achilles heel. Numbers were not his friend, and within one year of his "15 minutes of fame," he was yesterday's news.

As an aside, people usually figure this stuff out by the time they're 75 years old, but if you bought this book because of your entrepreneurial spirit, then you don't have the patience to wait until you're 75.

When people consider their strengths and their corresponding developmental considerations (what used to be referred to as potential limitations), they focus on their preferred or natural style of personality (Tier I). You may think some of my examples are less relevant to you at this time. Consider this: If I provide a list of ten suggestions to three people with the same personality, and ask each of them to determine which of the ten suggestions fit them, they would probably choose different suggestions. These differences occur because people learn from unique life's experiences; therefore, what may be an issue today will more than likely not remain an issue a year from now. Some learn sooner rather than later. Although some of these suggestions may not apply to you, before you disregard them, discuss them with someone who knows you well and whose opinions you respect.

This chapter provides you with information that won't only make you more effective in your current role, but will also offer concrete ideas for future opportunities, assignments, and roles. Ideally, you'll make a list of actionable items, devise an action plan, and begin to work toward making the changes necessary to become a better leader or manager. Read the following pages, which detail in depth the strengths and weaknesses of the seven personality types. Then absorb the content, create your Personal Action Plan, and determine the most appropriate plan of action – *for you*. I know – it's a difficult suggestion. But, remember, your development starts and ends with you.

Major Thought:

A number of books are available about discovering our strengths, suggesting we not worry about our limitations or weaknesses; just focus on strengths. While this paints a positive picture, the reality is we are hired because of our strengths, yet typically fired because of our weaknesses.

Trailblazers Strengths and Weaknesses

Trailblazers have an edge that can be the bane of their existence, as well as the source of their need for competition. They have a phenomenal ability to compete: They thrive on it, love it, and they're good at it. They enjoy working with systems, concepts, ideas, and technologies. They're technically oriented, have a strong strategic orientation, and are so results-oriented that they can easily forget about the people side of their business. That is a nice way of saying they have a tendency to step on toes. When working around a Trailblazer, wear your steel-toed shoes. These Generalists like to assume a role involving freedom of action within known structures, with strong leadership or competitive selling responsibilities. They have a need for autonomy and authority, and a predisposition toward communicating in a professional manner. Trailblazers are highly results-oriented, and carry a sense of urgency about setting and realizing goals. They also have an aptitude for keeping a variety of tasks on stream, and a preference for initiating projects under the defined parameters.

Trailblazers typically display a number of these qualities:

- Exhibits competitive, ambitious, and goal-oriented qualities
- Tackles projects aggressively
- Accepts responsibility and acts as an authority
- Resists objections and achieves goals in the face of obstacles
- Demonstrates ability to be logical, work-oriented, and analytical

> ### The Trailblazer Approach
>
> Rick Sapio of Mutuals.com has a Trailblazing personality. For years he lived in a hotel apartment suite that was in the same building as his Dallas office. He lived there because he wanted to focus on his business and no commute gave him that extra time and energy. He didn't have a television because he didn't want distractions. Rick did, however, have hundreds of business tapes and CDs and was surrounded by hundreds of motivational and business books. He wanted exclusive focus on his job. In his closet, he had 40 white shirts all in a row. With Rick's personality, delegating authority didn't come naturally. He was, however, able to hire another Generalist, specifically a Manager profile, to manage his day-to-day operations, thereby allowing himself the opportunity to work on the overall strategy and the big-picture side of his business.

Carving out a Niche

Trailblazers prefer being the driving force of an endeavor and, therefore, are typically the founders of many businesses. Instead of buying a franchise or a distributorship, they are more likely to start the company that competes with a franchise. Usually highly innovative; they see what Burger King does and subsequently imagines their operation becoming Burger King on steroids, but within their own environment. They're strong, calculating risk-takers who are willing to invest in themselves. They are purposeful in that they don't like to take "no" for an answer.

If Trailblazers don't surround themselves with those who can manage the people side, they'll run good employees away. They're known to alienate others and are so comfortable keeping things to themselves that they have only a few close friends. But it's nothing to worry about since they don't need many friends. The friends they do have are usually very close and maintained forever. Trailblazers can go months or years without connecting with their friends, but once they do, it's as if they were never apart.

If you want someone truly determined to get the job done, look to a Trailblazer, just don't worry about the bodies they leave in their wake. Trailblazers do best when they remember three important rules:

- Learn from developmental considerations

- Allow learned behaviors (Tier II) to take charge

- Mitigate my edge

Leverage Strengths for Greater Success

Action items for a Trailblazer are:

1. Take stock of your successes.
2. Conduct your own performance review.

Pushing for results is one strength of a Trailblazer.

- You are highly results oriented, ambitious, and assertive.
- You are unwavering in your desire to succeed.
- You are very comfortable expressing your point of view.

The strengths of most Trailblazers are typically found in individuals who...

- ...are extremely goal-oriented and take charge of situations.
- ...are very competitive and need to win.
- ...relish having authority and influence over others.

- …seek out challenges and tough problems to handle.
- …like to take risks and hold themselves accountable for the consequences.

To leverage your strengths, take stock of your successes. Think of the specific actions you took to achieve these results and recall situations where others helped along the way. Next time you face a challenge, draw on these experiences to guide you. Then conduct your own performance review. Where are you compared to your goals? Determine what you are doing well and look for areas where a different approach might be beneficial.

Turn Developmental Considerations into Advantages

Action items for a Trailblazer are:

1. Take a back-seat role.
2. Be the last to speak.

Collaborating with others is a developmental area for a Trailblazer.

- You want control and will automatically take over in many situations.
- You can be overbearing, discouraging input from others.
- You may be seen as dominant or self-centered.

To manage your developmental areas more effectively, take a back-seat role. Approach your next project with the idea that you don't have to take complete responsibility for the outcome. Instead, seek out the contributions of others and be prepared to share the credit with them.

Be the last to speak. In meetings, try not to influence the discussion too early on. Filter your comments by asking yourself, "Does this need to be said, or do I just *want* to say it?"

Go-Getters' Strengths and Weaknesses

Go-Getters have an ability to assume the role of a Generalist nature, with strong leadership or competitive selling responsibilities. They enjoy and have a need for autonomy and authority, as well as a clear preference for initiating and setting their own direction. Oriented toward achieving results, Go-Getters have a sense of urgency about setting and realizing goals and an aptitude for keeping a wide variety of tasks on stream.

Their predisposition toward persuasion allows them to diplomatically sell their ideas to others.

Go-Getters typically display a number of these qualities:

- Exhibit competitive, ambitious, and goal-oriented nature
- Tackle projects and situations aggressively
- Want responsibility for and authority over people
- Enjoy overcoming objections/resistance and achieving goals in the face of obstacles
- Show independence, persistence, and decisiveness

Carving out a Niche

Go-Getters work well in both ambitious and ambiguous environments. This means they can invest in, buy, or start a business that's new and unfamiliar to them. They don't require a high level of expertise in their endeavors. In their opinion, expertise is helpful, but not necessary. Being innovative, they're able to take others ideas to the next level. Constantly driven, they work well under pressure, multitask, and seem to be in constant motion. Go-Getters often have a chameleon-like quality that allows for a strong level of natural empathy. They are good collaborators and consensus-builders, and are a good source of motivation for themselves and others. A Go-Getter's influence is almost always positive.

Leverage Strengths for Greater Success

Action items for a Go-Getter are:

1. Encourage competition among your team.
2. Take charge of your personal development.

There's good news and bad news. The good news is that most people know how to identify their strengths. The challenge is they don't always understand that with each strength comes a corresponding and diametrically-opposed potential limitation.

Go-Getters' strengths are...

- ...extremely goal-oriented and take charge of situations.

- ...always competitive, need to win and thrive on overcoming obstacles to attain objectives.
- ...ideal for exerting authority and influence over others.
- ...obvious in seeking out challenges and tough problems to tackle.
- ...strategic risk-takers who are willing to be accountable for the consequences.

Competing is a strength of a Go-Getter

You enjoy winning and the success that comes with it.

- You seek opportunities to go head-to-head with others and will put a competitive spin on just about everything.
- You do not hesitate to take on new challenges, especially if the rewards and the risks are high.

To leverage your strengths, encourage competition among your team. You can increase productivity and get everyone engaged with a little healthy rivalry. Look for opportunities to beat the forecast – or your competitors.

Then, take charge of your personal development. Meet with your boss/coach to discuss how your job relates to the goals of the organization. Then, find out what you have to master in your current role to take it to the next level.

Go-Getters have an amazing level of self-confidence. Because of this, the Go-Getter is challenged in understanding how others can't do what he can so easily accomplish. A manufacturer of springs in the San Francisco Bay area (with a Go-Getter personality) has been growing his business at a double-digit clip for as long as anyone can remember. He refers to what he and his key people do as "the heavy lifting." This personality can do a lot of heavy lifting.

Turn Developmental Considerations into Advantages

Action items for a Go-Getter are:

1. Look for a team win.
2. Perform an unprovoked act of kindness.

Teambuilding is a developmental area for a Go-Getter.

- Your strong desire to "win the battle" may lead you to lose sight of the best solution.
- You may create long-term adversaries and discourage future alliances.
- You find it difficult to stay motivated when you do not feel personally challenged.

To manage your developmental areas more effectively look for a team win. When negotiating, rather than viewing a desired outcome in terms of, "What's in it for me?" ask instead, "What's in it for them?"

Perform an unprovoked act of kindness. For example, send a business opportunity to another division or volunteer to help an associate with whom you do not always see eye to eye. Create long-term allies who may help you down the road.

Once I knew a client's sales manager in a furniture store who was single, reasonably attractive, and a great closer. Many with the Go-Getter personality are great salespeople. On Saturdays when he was without a date for the evening and an attractive, single, female shopper was in the store, he was known to take the floor. He would make the sale, and then tell the store's new client that delivery typically took a week to ten days, but that if she were going to be home that night he would make arrangements to have the furniture delivered. He'd also bring the paperwork and a bottle of wine to celebrate her new purchase. Remember, I'm talking about potential limitations.

Managers' Strengths and Weaknesses

Managers have the ability to assume a Generalist role, with strong leadership or competitive selling responsibilities. Also, they have a need for autonomy and authority, a preference for initiating and setting their own direction, and a predisposition toward communicating in a professional manner. Managers have dispositions patient enough to cope with long-term projects and an inclination toward a day-to-day, evenly paced routine.

Managers typically display a number of these qualities:

- Exhibit competitive, ambitious, and goal-oriented nature
- Tackle projects and situations aggressively
- Want responsibility for and authority over people
- Enjoy overcoming objections/resistance and achieving goals in the face of obstacles
- Show independence, persistence, and decisiveness
- Want to take time to think things through

- Want to take charge and initiative
- Have the strength to follow through and perseverance to keep at it until they get results

Carving out a Niche

Managers have a strong technical orientation and are analytical, highly results-oriented, stable, methodical, patient, and somewhat independent. They like doing things on their own, are great behind-the-scenes leaders, and are great at working with systems, concepts, ideas, and technologies. They like to think things through. Their decision-making process might be described as "ready, aim, aim, aim, fire." Managers are loyal and strongly independent. They like to do what they feel comfortable with and dislike being swayed with any form of emotional argument. They enjoy working by themselves and could be challenged to manage those in a more active environment.

Leverage Strengths for Greater Success

Action items for a Manager are:

1. Find a mentor.
2. Go to bat for someone else.

Managers' strengths come from…

- …being extremely goal-oriented and stepping in to take charge of situations.
- …being highly competitive, needing to win, and thriving on overcoming obstacles to attain their objectives.
- …relishing their authority and influence over others.
- …seeking out challenges and tough problems to tackle.
- …being a risk-taker and holding themselves accountable for the consequences.
- …being very loyal as employees and employers.

Being assertive is a strength of a Manager.

- You have a great deal of confidence in your abilities.
- You have definite opinions and believe that your solutions and ideas are the best ones.

To leverage your strengths, find a mentor. Pick a person who has had a great impact on your company, someone who does a good job of influencing others while achieving consensus. Seek this person's advice the next time you have an idea you want to push through.

Then, go to bat for someone else. Use your assertive nature to help out team members who may be struggling with difficult situations.

1. Seek out challenges and tough problems to tackle
2. Like to take risks and hold themselves accountable for the consequences
3. Can be very loyal employees and employers

Asserting yourself is considered to be a strength of a Manager.

- You have a great deal of confidence in your abilities.
- You have definite opinions and believe that your solutions and ideas are the best ones.

Listening to others is a developmental area for Managers.

- You may not listen as well as you should.
- You often find yourself formulating your response before your colleagues have had a chance to finish and you can miss opportunities to get buy-in or build consensus.

To manage your developmental areas more effectively, listen actively. Look your colleagues in the eye and nod to indicate you understand their points of view. Start your response by summarizing what they have said. Never assume you know what someone is going to say before he says it.

Also, solicit feedback. Accept the fact that your ideas may not always be the best ones. Bounce them off someone you trust and listen to his opinions before moving forward.

An ongoing challenge for those with a Manager personality is the difficulty they often experience working with the people side of the business. They're so good with the technical side that their analytical nature overshadows their ability to work well with others. Loyalty is one of their assets, and the corresponding challenge can be best described by the following story.

I was presenting to a group of business owners in Oregon. One attendee had an especially strong Manager personality. I asked him if he is a creature of habit, and he said yes. I asked him whether his employees would consider him to be a highly loyal employer, and his answer again was yes. I asked him how long he'd been the CEO of the bank. He replied, "Fourteen years." And I finally asked how long he'd been thinking about firing someone but hadn't. He said, "About fourteen years now." In this case, loyalty becomes a limitation.

Motivators' Strengths and Weaknesses

Motivators have an ability to assume the role of a Generalist nature, doing best with leadership or selling responsibilities. They have an orientation toward achieving results and a sense of urgency about setting and realizing goals. They have an aptitude for keeping a wide variety of tasks on stream and a predisposition toward persuasiveness. They are able to sell their ideas to others in a diplomatic manner and cater to their need for autonomy and authority. Finally motivators have a preference for initiating and setting their own direction.

Motivators typically display a number of these qualities:

- Restless, driving, and energetic
- Strong sense of urgency to get things done quickly
- Work well under pressure and thrive on meeting tight deadlines
- Very friendly, sociable, and outgoing
- Work well with people, especially selling them ideas
- Good communicators
- Optimistic, tending to see the positive side of things

Carving out a Niche

Motivators do well in business with partners or in a business that involves others. In a service business, for example, their success can be based more on their location and concept than on the entrepreneur's directed approach to networking. Motivators can keep clients for life because they enjoy long-term relationships and are good at nurturing those relationships. They work well in a strong team environment and can find it somewhat challenging when it becomes confrontational. They have plenty of drive and multitask well, but can have a tendency to procrastinate.

Leverage Strengths for Greater Success

Action items for Motivators are:

1. Share your enthusiasm.
2. Examine the processes your company has in place.

Most Motivators…

- …are very restless, energetic, and take action quickly when things go wrong.
- …are change-oriented and enjoy new projects.
- …take a do-it-now approach.
- …set tight deadlines.
- …respond well to pressure.

Driving change is considered a strength of a Motivator.

- You are active and eager for new experiences.
- You have a strong and immediate need for action.
- You enjoy fast-paced environments where there is great activity.

To leverage your strengths, share your enthusiasm. You may be just the shot in the arm your peers need. Get your team to rally around a new idea – then be the one to step up and make things happen.

In addition, examine the processes your company has in place. There may be policies and procedures that have not changed with the times. Challenge them, but first take the time to understand them.

A friend and previous client, Mark Gordon, formerly residing in Washington D.C., had a data/wiring installation company. Mark struggled with holding others accountable, but he was wise enough to hire someone to handle the less enjoyable elements of his business. He concentrated on the business relationships, put together a buying group, eventually sold his business, and is now living in Florida working as a COO with an underwater salvage (treasure-hunting) company. He is living his dream by accomplishing his goals through others.

Turn Developmental Considerations into Advantages

Action items for Motivators are:

1. Eliminate surprises.
2. Look before you leap.

Staying focused is a developmental area for Motivators.

- You may not plan things in advance.
- You change focus quickly, making it difficult for others to keep track.
- You can get bored easily and are always looking for the next fire to put out.

To manage your developmental areas more effectively, eliminate surprises. Respect the fact that others may not share your sense of adventure. Make sure that everyone is on the same page prior to starting new activities.

Also, remember to look before you leap. Before jumping into something – and dragging everyone else in with you – take the time to think through the full ramifications of what you are about to do. List the pros and cons.

Authorities' Strengths and Weaknesses

Authorities and their Specialist counterparts make up more than 70 percent of the U.S. population. Remember America's beginning – our roots began with people who came to the New World seeking freedom, autonomy, independence, and control over their destinies. They were our founders, and in essence they were our earliest-day version of today's entrepreneurs. Authorities have the ability to function effectively in a specialized, expert role, with an aptitude for being a supportive team player, especially in a team-like environment. Their preference is to work within a clearly structured and closely supervised environment. Precise, detailed tasks, day-to-day, evenly paced routines, and a propensity for analyzing ideas, projects and tasks, accurately describe many Authorities. If you want something done right, give it to an Authority. They're great with the details and, therefore, are challenged by letting go – as no one will do it as well as they will. Better at delegating authority, their challenge is holding others accountable and dealing with confrontation. It's not that they can't deal with the difficult aspects of the business – they can – it just requires more effort.

Authorities typically display a number of these qualities:

- Accepting, cautious, and deliberate in approach
- Avoid friction with others
- Approach decisions cautiously
- Work well in teams
- Act in a conscientious and cooperative manner
- Respond well to details and take duties seriously
- Follow company rules and directions
- Remain relaxed, patient, steady, and reliable

Carving out a Niche

Authorities might refer to themselves as "accidental" entrepreneurs because they often end up running a business when that was never part of their original plan. Consequently, they're best served going into a business that embraces their level of expertise or allows them to develop a new level of expertise. Given their accommodating nature and dislike for prospecting, they need to be in a business where customers or clients are driven to them. In most cases, this personality type will either need a partner with a stronger natural sense of prospecting or networking, or have other Specialist-oriented personalities working and supporting them. Authorities can succeed in running someone else's business concept, such as a franchise or a distributorship, provided the organization is well supported with advertising and marketing.

Leveraging Strengths for Greater Success

Action items for Authorities are:

1. Encourage teamwork.
2. Provide upward support first.

Most Authorities...

- ...are agreeable and obliging when working with others.
- ...are careful to minimize risks before making decisions.
- ...are unpretentious and work to get things done without fanfare.
- ...foster a sense of harmony in the workplace and adopt compromise solutions.
- ...support team efforts.

Cooperating with others is a strength of an Authority.

- You like to keep the peace and will go out of your way to get along with others.
- You believe that teamwork is very important.
- You will take a collaborative approach on most issues.

To leverage your strengths, encourage teamwork. For example, do this by getting others to rally around a team member who has fallen behind. Or, approach it at a higher level, by helping your team understand the different ways your department supports the organization.

Provide upward support first. Be helpful in a way that will benefit you most. Be aware of your boss' needs, as well as those of other senior managers. Use your expertise to make them more productive.

T. Scott Gross is a professional speaker, author, restaurateur, and one hell of a great guy. A couple of years ago, Scott published the book *Why Service Stinks.* It is about the personalities that make the best customer service professionals. Scott has an Authority personality, yet his position requires a Go-Getter personality. If you consider his three positions along with his personality type, being a writer is a perfect fit. Being the front person for his restaurant, especially one that really believes in delivering great customer service, requires a Motivator personality – a stretch for an Authority. His third role as a keynote speaker is the one that requires the high dominance that's typical in a Go-Getter. When I first met Scott, he completed one of our personality assessments. When I presented him with his results, he categorically disagreed. He challenged, "How can I not be a risk taker? I fly planes. How can I not be a risk taker? I'm a volunteer paramedic. I save lives."

I asked him if he would ever consider taking off (flying) early in order to beat an approaching storm front. Would he ever take the steps he takes as a paramedic without having had training? A couple of weeks later he called and told me his reports were accurate. He's a great keynote speaker, but doesn't want anything to do with presenting a full-day program. Scott, on a daily basis – often several times a day – needs to stretch his personality so that he can effectively do all of his jobs. And a good job he does!

There are hundreds of examples of Specialists behaving like Generalists. It happens every day. It's not their natural style (Tier I), but due to their cognitive ability (Tier II) they understand the changes that are necessary for them to perform the (Tier III) actions.

The Specialist, when doing Generalist work, may very well be tired, even exhausted at the end of the day – but he *can* do the job. He can change his nature for short periods of time in order to have a greater impact on the position.

Turn Developmental Considerations into Advantages

Action items for Authorities are:

1. Create a "High Anxiety To-Do List."
2. Just say no.

Addressing adversity is a developmental area for Authorities.

- You can procrastinate when it's time to confront people or make difficult decisions.
- You are reluctant to voice your disagreement in group settings and will avoid rocking the boat.
- You can take on much more than is reasonable when supporting others.

To manage your developmental areas more effectively, create a "High Anxiety To-Do List." List the items that make you feel uneasy – for example, making a difficult decision, confronting an under-performing direct report or colleague, or selling your boss on a new idea – and make these a top priority.

Also, learn to say no. Resist your desire to pitch in when you have a number of time-critical tasks already. Stay focused on the tasks that help you achieve your goals.

Collaborators' Strengths and Weaknesses

Collaborators are another form of Specialists. They're cautious and deliberate and go out of their way to get along with others. They know they're part of a team and will work for the good of the group rather than seeking out individual recognition. They enjoy working in an environment with clear direction, and are so careful about making decisions that they must first conduct a thorough examination of the facts. They're great in new areas once they've developed the requisite level of expertise. Collaborators prefer a conflict-free working environment and will often try to mediate quietly, one-on-one, especially if co-workers are having problems with one another. They come across as thoughtful, sensitive, and caring people, and others will relate to them easily. Collaborators are accepting and cautious, and their challenge can be their desire to be liked at the expense of getting results.

Sociable and outgoing, they genuinely like people and enjoy working with them. They understand others, see their points of view, and get along well with them. Comfortable with people and confident in situations involving others, Collaborators are optimistic and tend to see the glass as half full. Good at making first impressions, they enjoy helping others. One of their challenges can be keeping the work environment professional.

Reliable and patient, they establish routines to complete their tasks. They work well with systems and methods and keep calm, cool, and collected most of the time. Predictable in performance, Collaborators are steady and consistent contributors. They don't feel the need to challenge the status quo and, as a result, tend to be a steadying influence on others. Frequent changes aren't necessary because they are comfortable working within the existing structure. Stable and dependable in approach, they like to pace themselves and develop their own work habits. Very loyal, Collaborators prefer a family-like environment. It is because of that high degree of loyalty, that they can find it difficult to confront employees and hold them accountable, let alone fire them.

Tending to be thorough, they tackle responsibilities conscientiously and enjoy preparing for contingencies. Collaborators follow directions and are good with detail. Of course, their difficulty with delegating details presents a challenge.

Collaborators typically display a number of these qualities:

- Accepting, cautious, and deliberate in approach
- Avoid friction with others
- Are good team members
- Approach decision-making cautiously
- Are good team members who are friendly, sociable, and outgoing
- Enjoys people, especially working with them

Carving out a Niche

It had better be about people, because Collaborators relish the people side of business. Consequently, they're well served in retail, customer service, or warm selling environments. They typically benefit by having a partner who is more aggressive about developing new business. Although Collaborators aren't usually comfortable with cold calling or pitching new ideas, they're far from pushovers and are adept at holding their ground when it comes to doing things right and following prescribed rules or guidelines.

They aren't big risk-takers and want to be sure they avoid blame, which is why doing things "right" is so important to them. They run a tight ship.

Leverage Strengths for Greater Success

Action items for Collaborators are:

1. Help others reach agreement.
2. Create alliances.

Most Collaborators...

- ...are agreeable and obliging when working with others.
- ...are careful to minimize risks before making decisions.
- ...are unpretentious and work to get things done without fanfare.
- ...foster a sense of harmony in the workplace and adopt compromising solutions.
- ...support team efforts.

    Building consensus is a strength of a Collaborator.

1. You take a safety-first approach to decision making and get buy-in before moving forward.
2. You collect input from others and work to accommodate their needs.

    To leverage your strengths, help others reach agreement. Your ability to seek compromise combined with your nonthreatening demeanor can be a great asset when egos start to clash.

    Also learn to create alliances. Let others know their opinions have been factored into the solution or have at least been considered. By developing allies, you will find it easier to have your positions accepted and to build confidence in your ability to make tough decisions.

Turn Developmental Considerations into Advantages

    Action items for Collaborators are:

1. Challenge your desire to get advice.
2. Present a solution.

Influencing others is a developmental area for Collaborators.

- Your efforts to gain acceptance from all sides can result in a watered-down solution.
- You may yield too much authority in areas where you are the expert.

To manage your developmental areas more effectively, challenge your desire to get advice. Next time you are about to seek input from others, first ask yourself if their contribution is necessary or whether you can make the decision yourself.

Present a solution. Rather than taking an open-ended approach to gathering input, start by proposing a solution. For example, start with, "Here's what I recommend. What do you think?"

Diplomats' Strengths and Weaknesses

Diplomats are driven individuals who get things done quickly, work well under pressure, and enjoy working with tight deadlines. They can adjust to change, are quick to respond to new situations, and work well in a changing atmosphere. They have a high sense of urgency, enjoying variety and working at top capacity. Diplomats enjoy it when things are really moving, and they can keep a variety of jobs going at once. Active and energetic, they vigorously attack the parts of the job they enjoy and push themselves and others to get results quickly.

Conscientious, they take their work seriously. Diplomats are good planners, and they like to be prepared for contingencies. Following directions carefully, they're thorough and good with detail. They respond well to guidance and direction. They learn the systems and procedures, becoming authorities in their field. Thorough and always putting their emphasis on the quality of their work, Diplomats adapt well to situations where they can do the work themselves and check details personally.

Sociable and outgoing, they genuinely like people and enjoy working with them. They understand others and see their points of view. They're optimistic and tend to see the positive side of things. At home with people and confident in situations involving others, Diplomats often make a good impression and enjoy helping others when possible. Outgoing and open, they're good communicators and relate well to others.

Tending to be good team players, they seek consensus in their dealings with others. They take a fairly careful approach to decision-making, preferring to examine available options before moving forward in an effort to avoid needless risks. Diplomats are inclined to respect authority, and they adjust well to supervision as long as it's fair and understanding.

The Diplomat is excellent working in retail or other people-oriented environments. For each strong point, though, there is a challenge. The Diplomat's challenges are as follows:

- May have difficulty holding others accountable
- May have difficulty dealing with confrontation
- May want to be liked at the expense of getting results
- May procrastinate
- May have difficulty letting go of details

Carving out a Niche

As Diplomats are both outgoing and empathetic, they often prefer to hold roles that support the leaders of an organization rather than being in charge themselves. Since they promote harmonious relationships and tend to be well liked, however, people are often happy and willing to follow their lead. The flip side of the coin is that Diplomats tend to avoid conflict and have a hard time asserting themselves and holding others accountable. Therefore, to be successful business leaders, they typically need to hire stronger, more results-oriented people to make sure that deadlines are met, commitments are kept, and staff members are following through on projects.

Leverage Strengths for Greater Success

Action items for Diplomats are:

1. Share your enthusiasm.
2. Examine the processes your company has in place.

Your responses are typical of individuals who...

- ...have a sense of urgency and are quick to react.
- ...like variety and enjoy taking on new projects.

- ...like pressure and deadlines.
- ...seek out fast-paced environments.

I recently worked with a Diplomat personality. She was a female franchisee in the early-childhood development industry. Her challenge was marketing the concept. The difference between the successful franchisees and those less so was mainly their ability to market. We devised a plan of action in which she and one of her employees visited with schools, church groups, day-care facilities, and other organizations. These were places where the parents of her potential students might congregate and, through the collective strength of both their personalities, they were able to successfully market their concept. Today, Gina is a very successful entrepreneur.

Responding urgently is a strength of a Diplomat.

1. You can quickly shift your focus to more critical priorities.
2. You are action oriented and want to do things now.

To leverage your strengths, share your enthusiasm. You may be just the shot in the arm that your peers need. Get your team to rally around a new idea, and then be the one to step in and make things happen.

Examine the processes your company has in place. There may be policies and procedures that have not changed with the times. You can look for ways to improve them, but first take the time to understand why they are there in the first place.

This is definitely one of the best customer-service or retail profiles you'll find anywhere. Diplomats are still Specialists, but they're great at building consensus and collaborating with others.

Turn Developmental Considerations into Advantages

Action items for Diplomats are:

1. Look before you leap.
2. Eliminate surprises.

Staying focused is a developmental area for Diplomats.

- You may jump in without taking the time to plan first.

- You can get bored easily and seek out new activities, making it difficult for others to follow.

To manage your developmental areas more effectively, look before you leap. Before jumping into something, take the time to think through the full ramifications of what you are about to do. List the pros and cons.

Eliminate surprises. Respect that others may not share your desire for something new. Make sure everyone is on the same page prior to starting new activities.

Strength and Weakness Self-Assessment

Based on what I've read in this chapter, I feel my strengths and developmental areas are most like:

Trailblazer _____
Go-Getter _____
Manager _____
Motivator _____
Authority _____
Collaborator _____
Diplomat _____
I also have qualities similar to: _____

Personal Action Plan

On the next few pages, you will begin to complete your Personal Action Plan.

- First, transfer the key strength or developmental area that you selected in the Self-Assessment, based on your personality type. If you were unable to find a match, then proceed by determining those items that you know to be your strengths or developmental areas.
- Then, use the suggested Action items to help you set concrete, on-the-job Action items.

For example, suppose your developmental area is "focusing on numbers" and your Action Item is to become more comfortable with numbers. Get to know percentages, dollar figures, and bottom-line financial details. Include any information that is important to success in your role and to your organization. Your own Action Item might translate into being prepared to make a better contribution at the next quarterly review. Study the YTD financials, and clarify any figures you don't understand with the controller. Your desired outcome might be to use any specific elements from the YTD financials in your presentation.

FIGURE 6.1: **Personal Action Plan-Strengths**

STRENGTH: USING LOGIC – Link your skills to strategy

DEVELOPING ON-THE-JOB ACTION ITEMS (Review the Action Items that will help you leverage this Strength.) • Personalize the Action Items related to the key strength you have selected or create your own Action Items below. • State your desired outcome.	TARGET DATE
1. Determine my best job fit, which is to be the front person, the person presenting, speaking, and developing the direction and strategic alliances. Be a rainmaker.	Done
2. Create the organization necessary to free myself of the day-to-day operations. To accomplish this I will need very strong key indicators, a comp plan to drive growth, engaged employees, and someone to take day-to-day operating responsibilities.	Ongoing process
3. Staff the organization with the skills necessary to allow me the opportunity to accomplish #1 listed above. This will include a great marketing person, a trainer, three salespeople and a solid administration team.	Ongoing process
4. Step out of the day-to-day operations, and select a Managing Director to manage the tactical side of the business. Don't sabotage them or yourself.	Done

POTENTIAL OBSTACLES (Identify any potential barriers to success)	WAYS TO OVERCOME OBSTACLES (How might you overcome these barriers?)
Inability to retain core personnel or their inability to perform at the level necessary to accomplish our goals.	Nurture our employees and become an employer of choice. Lead by example. Hold One-to-ones monthly so that I am not surprised by outcomes. Let people always know where they stand.

ASSESSING YOUR PROGRESS (To be completed once you have had the opportunity to implement your Action Plan.) How did it go? What was the outcome? In what ways could you further leverage this strength to achieve greater effectiveness?

Still struggling from our so-called recession. We laid off half our staff in 2009 and are now in the process of rebuilding. Hire one additional sales representative in the third quarter so they are ready for the IFA in February. Develop or acquire software for employee engagement studies.

FIGURE 6.2: **Personal Action Plan-Developmental Areas**

DEVELOPMENT AREA: COMMUNICATING YOUR MESSAGE – Anticipate Emotional Concerns and Put Yourself in Your Listener's Shoes

DEVELOPING ON-THE-JOB ACTION ITEMS (Review the Action Items that will help you manage this Developmental Area more effectively) • Personalize the Action Items related to the key developmental area you have selected or create your own Action Items below. • State your desired outcome.	TARGET DATE
1. Utilize Guinot's work in listening to what is being said, cognitively determine the motivation of the comment, and respond favorably eliciting greater feedback from the speaker. Don't become defensive, look for the best in others, and concentrate on what people are able to accomplish. Become a world-class teach of others (teach them to fish).	Ongoing
2. Use the objection process of Feel, Felt, Found. (i.e., I understand how you must be feeling. When I consider what you are saying, I have felt the same way when I experienced the same situation. What I found was…)	Ongoing
3. Develop procedures and systems to improve the training of others so that we can better measure their advancement, accomplishments, and understanding of the process…Embrace numbers and key indicators so that others know where they stand at all times and be engaged in mentoring or coaching them.	Ongoing

POTENTIAL OBSTACLES (Identify any potential barriers to success)	WAYS TO OVERCOME OBSTACLES (How might you overcome these barriers?)
My own stupid switch prevents me from accomplishing my goal. My drive and lack of patience get in my way, thereby causing me to be short with others	Interject more humor into the situation, don't take myself so seriously, and be patient with the speed at which others learn and process information.

ASSESSING YOUR PROGRESS (To be completed once you have had the opportunity to implement your Action Plan.) How did it go? What was the outcome? In what ways could you further develop this area to achieve greater effectiveness?
• Still struggling with #3 as we haven't yet begun tracking our metrics with the sales reps. I am paying much closer attention to the overall numbers including our P&Ls. • Goal for December is to have graphs that track the metrics posted.

FIGURE 6.3: Your Personal Action Plan – Strengths

STRENGTH:		
DEVELOPING ON-THE-JOB ACTION ITEMS (Review the Action Items that will help you leverage this Strength.) • Personalize the Action Items related to the key strength you have selected or create your own Action Items below. • State your desired outcome.		TARGET DATE
POTENTIAL OBSTACLES (Identify any potential barriers to success)		WAYS TO OVERCOME OBSTACLES (How might you overcome these barriers?)
ASSESSING YOUR PROGRESS (To be completed once you have had the opportunity to implement your Action Plan.) How did it go? What was the outcome? In what ways could you further leverage this Strength to achieve greater effectiveness?		

FIGURE 6.4: Your Personal Action Plan – Developmental Areas

DEVELOPMENT AREA: COMMUNICATING YOUR MESSAGE – Anticipate Emotional Concerns and Put Yourself in Your Listener's Shoes	
DEVELOPING ON-THE-JOB ACTION ITEMS (Review the Action Items that will help you leverage this Strength.) • Personalize the Action Items related to the key strength you have selected or create your own Action Items below. • State your desired outcome.	TARGET DATE
POTENTIAL OBSTACLES (Identify any Potential barriers to success)	WAYS TO OVERCOME OBSTACLES (What might you do to overcome these barriers?
ASSESSING YOUR PROGRESS (To be completed once you have had the opportunity to implement your Action Plan). How did it go? What was the outcome? In what ways could you further develop this area to achieve greater effectiveness?	

Chapter 6

— The Bottom Line —

➢ For each strength there is a corresponding and diametrically opposed developmental consideration (potential limitation).

➢ These potential limitations cause us to sabotage ourselves.

➢ We figure out this personality stuff usually by the time we are 75 years old. When we understand our personality from an objective perspective we can accomplish this understanding within the next 12 months. Are you ready?

➢ Each and every personality type has different and separate strengths and potential limitations.

➢ Failure to plan is planned failure. Take your time, complete your Personal Action Plan and update it often as you accomplish your goals.

➢ Refer to the Five-Tier Performance Pyramid and use your Personal Action Plan as an extension of your Tier III: Actions.

➢ Get yourself a coach or join a CEO/Entrepreneur Peer-to-Peer Group.

➢ We are hired because of our strengths and fired because of our limitations.

PART

II

How Entrepreneurs and Wantrepreneurs Operate

7

Entrepreneurs and Wantrepreneurs

What Drives Them

IT ISN'T NECESSARILY OBVIOUS THAT REWARDS LIKE MONEY TURN entrepreneurs and wantrepreneurs on. Indeed, most workers' motivational needs are rarely obvious.

Personality affects people's attitudes toward work according to Frederick Herzberg's theories on motivation. From his research, he concluded that such factors as company policy, supervision, interpersonal relations, working conditions, and salary are important, but not necessarily motivators. He believed the absence of these factors can create job dissatisfaction, but their presence does not necessarily guarantee motivation or create satisfaction.

Herzberg determined from his research that true motivators are elements that enrich a person's job. He found five factors in particular that are strong determinants of job satisfaction: achievement, recognition, the work itself, responsibility, and advancement. These motivators (satisfiers) are associated with long-term positive effects in job performance, whereas the basic factors (dissatisfiers) consistently produce only short-term changes in job attitudes and performance. Satisfiers describe a person's relationship with what he does, and many are related to the tasks being performed. Dissatisfiers have to do with a person's relationship to the context or environment in which he performs the job.

What makes entrepreneurs and wantrepreneurs tick? What motivates them, often against seemingly insurmountable odds? The answers to these questions are ego, status, sense of urgency, and independence. While successful business leaders make it look easy, there's more to their success than meets the eye.

You will no doubt relate to the motivational factors that are most in line with the type of entrepreneurial personality that you, or the entrepreneurs you know, possess. By looking at behind-the-scenes operations, thought processes, and strategies of successful entrepreneurs, you can discern what will work for you and how to leverage that knowledge and awareness. You will also find out where you might be tempted to compromise your integrity or get into trouble. Fortunately, I was able to learn some of these lessons in my youth, when the stakes were much lower.

Look at each of the four behavioral factors, as there are particular motivational needs for each:

- If I have a high level of Dominance then I am often motivated by independence, control, authority, autonomy, and a certain degree of power.
- If I have a high level of Sociability then I am typically motivated by recognition, being a part of a team, social stimulation, and being able to work with others.
- If I have a high level of Relaxation then I am motivated by things like stability, loyalty and working in an environment without a great deal of change.
- If I have a high level of Compliance then I will usually be motivated by security, understanding what is expected of me, having a book to go by, and being in an environment that is relatively free of risk. I want to be rewarded for my level of expertise.

Understanding one's motivation is important for increasing your own self-awareness, but also for increasing your awareness of what motivates others. Successful leaders have to know how to motivate others, especially others with complementary talents.

Lessons Learned

I was seven years old, and it was a warm Spring day in Peoria, Illinois – with blankets of colorful flowers blooming all over the neighborhood. It was also opening day of a new Spudnut Donut shop at the corner of University and Main. I became an avid customer and, with my loyal visits, the owner immediately took a liking to my chutzpah. He made me an offer I couldn't refuse: two donuts and $4 a day to deliver free donut samples to the neighborhood. This was his way of attracting the neighbors to his new store. Pretty good idea; I'm still a big believer in sampling.

I started on a Saturday morning and delivered doughnuts for several blocks, giving away more than 50 a day. All the neighbors loved the idea – so much so that they started giving me tips for the service. Sometimes they paid me as much as 50 cents.

The second week, I was caught in a dilemma. The neighbors, becoming accustomed to the service, wanted to pay for the doughnuts rather than going to the doughnut store. So here I am with my 50 sample doughnuts, $4 a day from Mr. Spud-nut, and a thriving doughnut business, supplying customers ready to pay top dollar. Well, I'm sure you can see the dilemma from a seven-year-old's perspective. What would you do?

Trailblazers' Motivation

The Trailblazer is the granddaddy of all Generalists. Trailblazers are doggedly determined to get their own way and equally focused on results. They're much more analytical than their more sociable Generalist counterparts. Therefore, their Achilles heel is the people side of business; they're much more apt to enjoy focusing on the number side.

With a strong focus on winning, they promote internal competition and set genuinely ambitious, challenging goals with short time frames. Emphasizing quantifiable results, they communicate their ideas in a straightforward, bottom-line manner. They're careful to keep a professional distance from their people except when a more congenial approach is essential to attaining their business goals. Although they can be patient coaches when warranted, they can also light a fire under their team when appropriate. They expect their team to follow defined parameters, although they accept some innovation.

They want constant challenge, control and room to maneuver. They want their accomplishments to be recognized both publicly and tangibly. They process information largely by using logic, keeping to the facts, and making sure they understand people ramifications. They hold their emotions in check and keep things moving as they set their own deadlines. They want some variety in their jobs in order to keep from becoming bored. They follow rules, especially if they have a part in setting the rules.

Managing the Trailblazer

In Accord Management System's consulting practice, we need to hire a diverse group of personalities. Most are Generalists, and one of the most difficult to manage is the Trailblazer personality. Their favorite question is "Why?" as they challenge everything. They have the capacity to be somewhat, if not very, difficult to manage. The good news is that they are great at business development. The better news is that if you know they are going to be challenging, then it becomes easier to direct them. Tell them what you want, give them the tools, and get out of the way. If they are willing to keep you informed, then you have done very well.

Many of the entrepreneurs you hear about are Trailblazers. That's because they're able to make the difficult decisions that often affect their employees adversely. These are the CEOs or entrepreneurs who are able to lay off their entire workforce to break a union effort. They don't enjoy confrontation, but they don't avoid it either. You probably don't want to negotiate with Trailblazers, because they rarely lose. Their primary style of negotiation is a "win at all costs" approach that is often mitigated by a nice compromise or more conciliatory style. They can appear to come across as warm and friendly, but don't let your guard down – they'll take you to the proverbial mat.

Many of our clients have a Trailblazer personality. They're often the founders of their destiny and seldom embrace the ideas of others. You won't find many Trailblazers serving as franchisees, but you will find them in the ranks of the franchisors.

Within the corporate environment, Trailblazers usually occupy positions that are more analytical, such as those of distribution and production managers. They're the CEO, the CFO, the COO, the CIO, the CTO, and the E-I-E-I-O. (A little humor.)

What Works and What Doesn't

When working with or managing Trailblazers, *do*:

- Challenge them to excel and set stimulating goals, or they will become bored very easily.
- Build accountability into their role. They don't mind playing by the rules; they just want to have input.
- Communicate with them from a logical perspective, and keep to the facts because they do not want to be swayed by emotional argument. They, as most introverts, have tremendous capacity for making extroverts absolutely crazy.

- Be professional in your dealings with them, as they don't warm up to others quickly or easily. Once they trust you, they will do almost anything for you.
- Involve them as a sounding board to test the validity of an argument or a case you're developing, but be careful what you ask for. They can be so analytical that they came across as being terse or rude.

If you don't do these things, they will make your life miserable.

I asked a client I was working with, "When was the last time you screwed up a people decision?" He replied, "There was a time when I wasn't a very effective manager. It may have been as recent as this morning. I know I have cost myself literally hundreds of thousands of dollars largely because of my need to control. I need to control the outcome, the process, and yes, even the people." This need to control has caused very talented and capable employees of Trailblazers to seek their opportunity elsewhere. I am sure this client created much of his own competition.

When working with or managing Trailblazers, *do not*:

- Control their activities too closely. They enjoy freedom and will fight for it.
- Demand that they report every little detail to you. They prefer to be measured on overall results. They are willing to perform to metrics as long as they are playing on a level playing field.
- Compliment them unless there's a good reason. They aren't comfortable with superficialities as they think you are up to something. They don't mind compliments, but they prefer them in private.
- Get upset if they are a little less than diplomatic. Sometimes they let their intensity obscure the possible impact on others. Their style of communication is somewhat matter of fact and strictly business, to the point where they can be considered rude. It is important to know that they usually aren't rude; it just comes across that way.

Trailblazers are very creative and strong advocates of their own ideas, so don't become defensive if they constantly want to change things. They naturally look for different solutions.

Go-Getters' Motivation

With a strong focus on winning, Go-Getters promote internal competition and set genuinely ambitious, challenging goals with short time frames. Focusing on outcomes rather than processes, they maintain a more or less hands-off approach and are generally comfortable with delegating the "how" to their staffs. They share their excitement with their teams and motivate those around them to fast action. They are good mentors for their teams and they gather input from those around them. They share their knowledge, encourage others to do the same, and provide positive feedback when needed.

Go-Getters are looking for constant control and the room to maneuver. They want their accomplishments to be recognized—both publicly and privately. They'll set ambitious goals and targets for themselves. They have strong convictions and want to do things their own way. They want to know that they're in control. They may occasionally need to be refocused. Go-Getters may also disagree with an idea unless they are part of the thought or unless it is presented by someone they truly respect. They work well under pressure and keep things moving; as such, they prefer a variety of assignments and don't want too much routine. They want interaction with others and desire a higher-than-average level of social stimulation. Go-Getters are an awesome force as long as they get their way. Remember that their motivational needs are independence, control, authority, autonomy, and a certain degree of power.

A CEO client by the name of Tom once told me a story about the time he was a sales manager in a fast-growing company. He was next in line for the general manager's position. Tom had been on board for just about a year when the previous general manager prematurely retired. Tom wasn't ready for the position—or so the owner thought—and the promotion went to one of Tom's peers, who proceeded to micro-manage Tom. (If you were being micromanaged, how long would you stay?) Tom was gone within 60 days and went to work for the competition. That is where the story takes an amazing turn. The company that Tom went to work for was in the same industry as his previous employer. Tom's new company grew largely through acquisitions. One of the first companies it acquired was Tom's old company, and the first person that Tom fired was...well, you get the story.

What Works and What Doesn't

When managing Go-Getters, *do*:

- Challenge them to excel, and set stimulating goals, because they love to play the game and always play to win.

- If there's room for advancement, make sure they're aware of the potential. Not everyone wants to get ahead, but Go-Getters typically do. Because of this trait, it can be challenging to keep them motivated and focused.
- Entrust them with authority. They will look at your company as their own and, as long as they maintain this perception, they will stay.
- Urge them to delegate some of the more intricate details. This becomes a real challenge for Go-Getters because they can handle the intricate details; they just don't enjoy them. Again, if you maintain their buy-in, they will handle the details.
- Acknowledge their contributions when you act on one of their suggestions. It makes them feel they are being appreciated and that goes a long way in motivating them.
- Build strategies with them so they can stay in focus.

Sally, a CEO client of mine, met with her Director of Sales at least once everyone six months. Meetings were scheduled specifically to determine and maintain the employee's focus. The last thing Sally did at every meeting was ask if the Director of Sales still bought into her vision. She felt she was able to keep him years beyond her expectations. In order to forestall his departure, she opened a subsidiary with him at the helm. She had designed a set of golden handcuffs.

When working or managing Go-Getters, *do not:*

- Encroach on their authority. They're protective of their autonomy. Actually they are protective of just about everything. They can be territorial when necessary.
- Take credit for their ideas/work. Recognition is important to them. There is no quicker way to get a Go-Getter to quit than to take credit for his accomplishments. On the other hand, now you know how to get one to quit.
- Let them get away with anything they shouldn't; they are okay with accountability. Their independence just gets the better of them at times.
- Hesitate to stand up to them when necessary. They might need reminding that their way isn't always the best. (It helps to show good reasons why.) Just be careful how you go about it. They are not fond of public criticism but, then again, I don't know too many people who like it.
- Be insincere. They can accept the good and the bad in people.

Managers' Motivation

The Four-Penny Technique

When coaching, I use the four-penny technique. It works well for all analytical leaders because it provides them with a metric to gauge their Tier II and Tier III actions. Also, it helps them work better with others. Start every day with four pennies in your right pocket. By the end of the day, your job is to have four positive conversations with four different employees. With the completion of each conversation move one penny from your right pocket to the left pocket. By the end of the day, all four pennies should be in your left pocket. A positive conversation should take less than 60 seconds. One last thought: A comment or compliment must not end with the word "but."

With a strong focus on winning, Managers have personalities very similar to their Go-Getter cousins in that they promote internal competition and set genuinely ambitious, challenging goals. Focusing on the outcome rather than the process, they maintain a more or less hands-off approach, generally comfortable with delegating the "how" to their staffs. With an emphasis on quantifiable results, they communicate their ideas in a straightforward, bottom-line manner. They're careful to keep a professional distance from their people except when a more congenial approach is essential to attain their business plan goals. In their own way, Managers show a good deal of patience when working with and coaching others, even while maintaining an arm's-length relationship.

Managers want to be challenged, as well as to have control and opportunity to express their ideas. They typically have strong metrics that support and guide their goals. They look at their numbers on a daily basis and are strong cause-and-effect thinkers. They have firm convictions and will insist on doing things their own way. They need to feel they're in control, and they can get downright cranky when they've lost it. Managers can be respectful of authority, especially if they sense they've made an error. All they want is for others to explain their position logically. They keep to the facts and attempt to make sure they understand the people ramifications, all the while keeping their emotions in check. They prefer having the chance to think things through and, if there's an emergency, they want to be notified as soon as possible. They want to hear the bad news before it happens and the good news after it happens. They hate surprises.

Managers are doggedly determined to win, but they approach their world from a rather analytical and methodical perspective. They don't say much, but what they do say is usually important. One of my clients is Frank, a minority owner of a $20 million-a-year implementer of computer systems. In 2005, Frank's company installed a new accounting package. I've learned such packages should run in tandem with existing packages for a minimum of three months, i.e., both accounting packages should run simultaneously to make sure there are no glitches. Frank's controller did not recommend this, and about six months later, the company discovered that its bank account had $500,000 less than it should have. One accounting package looked at invoicing and collections differently than the other.

The challenge for Frank was, and continues to be, that he and his majority partner have almost the same personality. Frank wants his independence and his partner wants to maintain his control. Frank is an introvert and so is his partner. Frank is a loyal person who doesn't want to be rushed into making decisions, just like his partner. That loyalty is their saving grace; they're both high in the loyalty index and not quick to change the status quo. Both Frank and his partner were wise enough to bring in a third-party business coach. This professional forces each of them to sit down once a month and bring their issues to the surface, working with them to mitigate their respective edges – and boy do they have them.

There are several great coaching organizations you may want to consider. At one time I was a member of Vistage, a peer-to-peer group for CEOs. I attended monthly meetings, but the most important aspect of my membership is that I have a one-on-one with my chair every month where we discuss my issues. His job is to hold me accountable.

What Works and What Doesn't

You will notice that the Manager is very similar to the Trailblazer. The only difference is the Manager's level of relaxation. When managing or working with Managers, attempt to provide the following:

- Because of their analytical style, it is important to coach them to adopt a team perspective. This is not easy for Managers because they prefer to handle the heavy lifting themselves.
- They have been accused of being somewhat opinionated and stubborn; therefore, it is important to resolve your differences privately, but together.

> **Highly Driven Meets Relaxed**
>
> If you are highly driven and are comfortable working under pressure, then you may have difficulty developing and maintaining an appreciation for those who are more relaxed. The challenge that you as a leader have is developing an appreciation for why others can't do what you can so easily accomplish.

- Communicate with them from a logical perspective, and keep to the facts. Emotional argument is lost on them, as are many of the nuances that more social individuals might possess.
- They prefer working on their own, so provide as many opportunities for them to fly solo as possible. Also, inform them that if they plan to grow in your organization, they'll need to learn to work by with and through others.
- Managers are somewhat private individuals and professionalism is important to them. Do not take liberties or get too touchy unless you're looking for a harassment issue. Respect Managers' privacy.
- Remember – they are creatures of habit who enjoy the stability of their lives. They would never choose a chaotic environment, so do what you can to maintain a stable workplace.

When managing or working with a Manager, do yourself a favor and *do not*:

- Expect them to become instant friends. They prefer taking their time to get to know someone. Once you become a member of their inner circle, feel confident that they will go to the mat for you. (Or, in non-sports terms, they take care of those that take care of them.)
- Compliment them unless there's a good reason. They aren't comfortable with superficialities.
- Get upset if they're a little less than diplomatic. They sometimes let their intensity obscure the impact of their analytical skills. This is because they prefer dealing with the technical side of the business more than the people side.
- Don't put pressure on them unnecessarily. Managers have a high level of relaxation, and with this can come the desire to be given as much notice as possible when things are about to change. They function best in a calm, predictable environment. You don't have to go overboard on this, just provide as much advance notice as possible.
- Leave everything until the last minute. Be sure to respect their need to schedule tasks methodically.

Motivators' Motivation

The Motivator is a Generalist with high dominance, high sociability, and both drive and independence. Motivators are encouraged by internal competition and enjoy challenging yet attainable goals. They aren't as aggressive as Go-Getters or Managers, but they're very energetic. They'll light a fire under their teams, motivating them to immediate action. Sympathetic and empathetic, they understand their staff members' individual concerns and get buy-in or agreement accordingly. Motivators share their knowledge and are genuinely interested in mentoring, providing positive feedback, and maintaining an atmosphere that encourages personal growth and empowerment.

Motivators keep things moving and use their sense of urgency to get things done quickly. They work well with deadlines, always putting pressure on themselves. They are also comfortable putting others under the same pressure. Make sure they finish what they start, because they can have a tendency to go off on tangents. This is a challenge faced by all people with low levels of relaxation. They multitask well, work well under pressure, and are very flexible. But the flip side is they may have a tendency towards procrastination and can find constant focus challenging. There's no lack of distractions for Motivators. They need to interact with others and like being asked for their insights about the people side of the business. Don't give them too many projects where they have to work alone, because they tend to excel in environments with a high level of social stimulation. Challenge them, let them set some of their own goals, and give them the freedom to accomplish those goals.

Jay Sweet is the CEO of Boyd Lighting in San Francisco, a family-owned business. Having a Motivator personality puts him in a great position to sell and market his company and himself. Remember the first scene in *Mr. and Mrs. Smith* where there was a shoot-out? Remember the beautiful lighting fixture that was destroyed in a hallway, riddled with bullets? That fixture was one of Jay's products. He knows people, appreciates them, and is a tremendous motivator, hence the title – Motivator.

Boyd Lighting is very entrepreneurial company. It would almost be impossible to succeed in a creative endeavor unless you have the drive to push for results. Because of Jay's high level of sociability, he knows almost everyone in the industry. If a designer has a new idea, Jay will be one of the first people he contacts.

What Works and What Doesn't

The Motivator is similar to the Go-Getter, except his dominance and sociability are reversed; that is, he usually enjoys the people side more than the technical side of business.

When managing or working with Motivators, remember the following:

- The Motivators are great at keeping a number of projects on track, so give them the opportunity to work on a wide variety of projects simultaneously.
- One advantage driven people have is how well they work well under pressure. Because of that, they can have a tendency to go off on tangents. Usually, they will be open to the relationship where, together, a strategy is built for them to stay in focus.
- Motivators are usually great communicators. Make the most of their ability to communicate by seeking their insights into people. They can be great in sales or management roles as long as they are working with others.
- The Motivator personality has been called a behavioral barometer. You can feel comfortable seeking or soliciting their input, as they are often accurate gauges of office morale.
- Depending on the relationship between their dominance and independence, you can feel comfortable providing opportunities for them to make decisions. As their dominance gets closer to the norm line, they will have less concern about making the decisions themselves.

When managing or working with Motivators, *do not*:

- Assign them too many routine, repetitive tasks. They get bored quickly and have to work at maintaining their focus. It becomes a challenge for the innovative CEO because Motivators *always* want to do more.
- Dampen their enthusiasm by prohibiting their occasional tangents. Sometimes those tangents can produce unexpected options.
- Object if they let things go until the last minute, as long as they bring it in on time – and no quality has been lost. They work best under pressure. Why do many of us wait until the last minute to complete our projects? It is because we can.

My grandmother was a Motivator, and she was the one who lent me the money to go to college. Naturally, my first approach for financing was our neighborhood banker. The bankers were cordial enough because Grandma was an important customer, but I had no collateral and was turned down—can't blame them. So I approached Grandma. She said she'd lend me the money, and I gallantly suggested that she charge me interest. She agreed and said, "How about 10 percent?" Astonished, I told her I could borrow the money from the bank at only 5 percent. (It was a long time ago.) She said, "Then perhaps you should borrow the money from the bank." I chose the 'Bank of Grandma' and after graduating from college it took me years to pay off the loan. When my grandmother passed away, I was notified that the entire amount of the loan, plus the 10 percent and compound interest, was sitting in a special account with my name on it. Grandma was a pretty sly lady.

The Role Self-Awareness Plays

People can understand and predict how Motivators, Managers, Go-Getters, and Trailblazers find their success, but what about the other 70 percent of the population? They are able to achieve success (you noticed I didn't say, "enjoy a similar success") by knowing the behaviors necessary to being successful (Tier II). Once they understand the right behaviors, they must define and take the right actions (Tier III) and accurately measure those actions (Tier IV) to achieve the right results (Tier V).

Embracing Change

We make the concept of change sound easy. For the most part, embracing change is an easy process to follow. The real difficulty comes when you start doing it. Knowing the behaviors we need to change is simple; we hear these messages daily: lose weight, exercise more, work harder, relax more. The lifelong challenge is turning these behavioral expectations into actions. Based on my experience, one defining factor of motivation is passion. Those that have and maintain passion for what they do have all the motivation one could ever want.

Now it's time to look at the personalities that are more wantrepreneurial. These are the Specialist or experts. They prefer having structure, are motivated by security and stability, and are more risk-adverse. But success need not elude them. They can be very successful.

Authorities' Motivation

Authorities lead by example, focus on output and seek consensus. They are willing to subordinate their own agendas for the good of the whole, striving to eliminate controversial situations. Focused on getting the job done as it should be, they seek well-defined, formal parameters for themselves and their staff, ensuring that proper procedures are understood and followed. In their own quiet way, they show great patience when coaching others. They're loyal and work hard to ensure that their teams can progress at a comfortable pace. Authorities communicate their ideas in a rational, straightforward way. They prefer to maintain some professional distance, concerned that becoming too friendly might hamper their ability to treat their teams objectively.

They prefer being subject-matter experts. They like others to show their appreciation for their contributions and provide strong support when and if they ask for it. Authorities don't make tough decisions easily or readily. They prefer to have enough facts to allow them to prepare thoroughly. Wanting to know what's expected, they dislike dealing with ill-defined projects. Good at setting their own pace, they prefer for others to take their time when explaining things, in order to fully answer their questions. They want things around them to remain as calm as possible, especially if they can maintain their routines. They want time to prepare and really keep their emotions in check.

Authorities are rarely the founders of their enterprises, but they're often the franchisees, the distributors, or the second- or third-generation entrepreneurs. They just do it differently.

Several years ago, I was giving a presentation to a group of entrepreneurs in New York City. The topic was personality and leadership. In preparation for the presentation, I surveyed the personality of each attendee and their respective key executives. One member, with an Authority personality, approached me after the presentation and asked whether I would consider hiring someone with his personality as a CEO. I said, "No." He wasn't surprised. He wasn't too wild about his position, considered himself to be an accidental CEO, and was, in fact, a second-generation entrepreneur. Interestingly enough, he was successful. His business generated about $3 million in annually revenue. He enjoyed the financial side of the business and the manufacturing or outsourcing side, but he didn't care for the sales or people side. Also, he didn't like confrontation or holding others accountable. Therefore, he hired only those that were easy for him to manage: other Specialists. There you have the problem.

I presented to this same group a couple years ago, and the same CEO approached me before the meeting and asked whether I remembered him. I did, largely, because I'd met with his mentor the night before and discussed his success. Paul was the benefactor of ongoing coaching and, because of this, he'd hired a great vice president of sales—one with the right personality. The CEO granted him the necessary authority to make decisions and the autonomy to enjoy his position, and today they have annual revenues in excess of $25 million.

Paul was able to develop the behaviors necessary to be an excellent CEO because he knew who he needed to become to accomplish his goals. Even better, he was able to hire those who could make him successful. Letting go of the details was and still is his challenge. Coaching helped Paul get around this through an agreement he had with his VP of sales. Paul agreed to allow his VP to exercise his authority and autonomy, in exchange for constant updates on performance, pricing, and other issues that were important to him. The more the VP was able to do this, the less important it became. Both parties won – cool!

What Works and What Doesn't

When managing or working with Authorities, it is important to recall the following:

- As Specialists, the Authorities want to understand exactly what is expected, so be sure to reach agreement with them on their specific goals.
- They like to make carefully considered decisions. Provide them with the environment that allows for this contemplation.
- Authorities are relatively serious individuals. Management should actively solicit their perspective in meetings and rely on their specialized focus. They will see a side of issues that others may miss.
- They are very dependable workers. Thus, you can count on them to follow through carefully. If I were an astronaut going up in the space shuttle, I would want an Authority installing the "O" Rings in the Space Shuttle.
- Sometimes Authorities can make managers crazy, especially Generalist managers. It is important to spend the time necessary to answer their questions about how a specific project or task should be done. Their favorite question is, "How?"

When managing or working with Authorities, be sure you *do not*:

- Put Authorities in positions where they have responsibility for difficult people. They don't want to make tough people decisions, unless they absolutely must; however, they won't enjoy it.
- Give them vague instructions. They prefer specifics.
- Expect them to make big decisions quickly or easily. They base their decisions on solid research and clearly defined rules. Yet, if doing something the right way is important, you definitely want an Authority working on the project.
- Give them too many things at once. Because of their high level of relaxation, they prefer to finish a project before beginning another.

Collaborators' Motivation

The Collaborator is another Specialist personality. The difference between Collaborators and Authorities is that Collaborators have a higher-than-average level of sociability. They're able to build consensus, motivate their employees, and work with and through others. They can "sell" easily, provided they're selling to a warm market where the customer is attracted to their location, brand, or possibly tenure in the business or area of expertise. An example of this type of position would be a convenience-store operator. The difference between a national brand such as Circle K or 7-Eleven, and its local competition, is that the national brand may generate twice the annual revenue based largely on brand awareness and the standards it maintains, like similarities of store layouts. (There's something safe in knowing what to expect.) This is of tremendous benefit to Specialists' personalities because their success may be more dependent brand or location than on their personality.

In the previous best seller, *Follow this Path,* (Warner Business Books, 2002), the authors (Curt Coffman and Gabriel Gonzalez-Molina) say, "Customers are five times more likely to return to a specific location because of the people who work there." When the Collaborator is the one running the store, return business is almost a lock. It's the Collaborator's extra bit of sociability that makes the difference.

Collaborators lead by example, focus on the team, and seek consensus. They are willing to subordinate their own agenda for the good of the whole, and strive to eliminate clashing situations. They concentrate on inspiring team cooperation. Collaborators share their knowledge and are interested in both mentoring and encouraging an atmosphere of personal growth. They show a good deal of patience when working with and coaching their team. They strive to make sure that they and their team can prepare for contingencies at a reasonable pace. Also, Collaborators set parameters for their staff, always careful about ensuring proper procedures.

Collaborators want to become subject-matter experts. They want to be appreciated for their contributions, and they may want strong support. They don't make tough decisions readily, nor are they fond of unnecessary pressure. Collaborators enjoy interacting with others and feel valued when their opinions are shared; as such they don't want to be too isolated. It's important for others to recognize that some things may not be that urgent and that Collaborators don't embrace multitasking. They want all the information they need before making decisions. Their preference is to ask their questions in advance, occasionally seeming to expect too much detail.

At Accord Management Systems, we have hired Collaborators on our staff. They are absolutely wonderful because they will do whatever is necessary to do it right. The more thorough the managers are, the better the Collaborators they will become. You will find that Collaborators are highly energetic and truly loyal. They enjoy working with clients and, most importantly, they always want to do a good job. If you embrace personality testing, you can find Collaborators to support your business.

What Works and What Doesn't

You will notice that the difference between Collaborators and Authorities is their level of sociability. From an entrepreneurial perspective, this can be a dramatic advantage because the Collaborator is able to use this sociability to sell, convince, and manage.

When managing or working with Collaborators, *do:*

- Be specific, reach agreement with them, and make sure the Collaborator understands the expectations and specific goals.
- Keep their trust. The Collaborator personality has a tendency to want to do things right and to keep things professional. They build their relationships over time and trust is an important part of that foundations.
- Minimize their deadlines and changes due to their high relaxation. Also, be sure to explain why the change is necessary.
- Make sure they understand their roles in relation o the project as a whole. Because of their expertise, they may have some good alternatives and ideas.

When working with or managing Collaborators, *do not:*

- Give them vague instructions unless you want to make them crazy. They prefer specifics. The challenge for most Collaborators is that they often end up working for or with a Generalist. This can make all parties frustrated unless each understands what makes the other tick, as well as what ticks the other off.
- Give them responsibility for difficult people. They don't want to make tough people decisions. Most Specialists are more authorities in their management styles. Collaborators have a particular challenge in that they also have high levels of sociability, and this factor can create additional stress if they want to be liked at the expense of getting results.

- Let them feel as if they're out on a limb. Be sure they have the support they need. They like to know they have backup.

Diplomats' Motivation

Diplomats prefer to lead by example and enjoy focusing on team spirit. They seek consensus and work to eliminate conflict as much as possible. They use their own need for speed to demonstrate the appropriate response time to their staff. Diplomats set well-defined, formal parameters for their staff, ensuring that the proper procedures and boundaries are clear. They concentrate on inspiring team cooperation. Also, they share their knowledge, and are interested in mentoring and in encouraging an atmosphere of personal growth.

They keep things moving and prefer to set their own deadlines. They want a variety of assignments and don't appreciate having too much routine. They'll check details and follow through to make sure they're handled correctly and thoroughly. Don't expect them to make big decisions by themselves – they prefer to build consensus when making their decisions. Diplomats won't appreciate being too isolated. They want to specialize and make sure they have the opportunity to do things right. They want whatever information is pertinent to their success, so don't let them feel as if they're on their own.

From an entrepreneurial perspective, the Diplomat is the king of the Specialists; he has all the right things going on. Diplomats have the sociability to handle the customers and employees alike. They have the drive to put pressure on both themselves and others. They have the compliance to ensure that the details of the business are handled in a satisfactory fashion. Their challenge is that they're tactically oriented, which means they won't typically be the founders of businesses, but they can be great at running retail operations. Do you have any idea how many retail franchise opportunities exist? Lots! Remember, though, there is a difference between running a franchise where customers are attracted to the national brand versus owning an individual retail store.

Successfully operating an independently owned retail location could be much more challenging because the Diplomat would be responsible for the marketing and networking, areas more associated with the Generalist personality. It's not that they can't handle the Generalist expectations, it can just be more stress and challenge than they want.

A number of years ago a friend by the name of Gary asked me to teach him my business. I told him it really took a strong Generalist personality to be successful in my line of work. I had known Gary for a number of years, and asked me repeatedly. Finally, I relented and told him he could join me on a training trip to Charlotte, North Carolina. Everything was fine until the first morning. We were in downtown Charlotte. It was beginning to rain, and we were ready to cross the street when I realized that Gary was not walking with me. I turned around, walked back to Gary, whose feet appeared to be cemented to the curb, and said, "Let's go. What are you doing?" He said, "There is a police officer in his car and I don't want to get a jaywalking ticket." This actually happened. I then said, "Gary, it's raining, let's go." Gary walked to the corner, waited for the light to change, and then crossed. Those were the behaviors of a Specialist, specifically a Diplomat.

What Works and What Doesn't

When working with or managing Diplomats, *do:*

- Provide a fast-changing environment. They can handle a number of different projects provided they have the right level of expertise. If they know what they're doing, then they can handle it – as well as enjoy a fast pace.
- Give them a well-defined, clear structure. As Specialists, the better their understanding of the expectations, the better they are able to perform.
- Make them an integral part of almost any team. The Diplomat is a great leader of other Specialsts.
- Remember they are "how" people and want to make carefully considered decisions.

When working with or managing Diplomats, *do not:*

- Assign them too many routine, repetitive tasks. They get bored quickly.
- Become defensive if they constantly want to change things. They naturally look for different solutions.
- Expect results before they've finished the project. Their thorough approach requires that they complete assignments fully.
- Ask for decisions in areas outside their expertise. Instead, let them become your expert advisors.
- Give them vague instructions. They prefer specifics.

- Put them in situations where they have responsibility for difficult people. They don't want to make tough people decisions.

Authorities' Blame Game

I have discussed how people come in different flavors, which includes their choice of questions or words. The more compliant Specialists have a tendency to be more concerned with the "how" side of the business. If they know how, then they can do it right. If they do it right, they avoid blame. Simply stated, Authorities will do anything they can to avoid blame. The challenge is they often work for or with a Generalist personality who is primarily a "why" person. To bring this story full circle, the Authority asks the Generalist how he wants a project done, and the Generalist says, "Don't worry about how to do it. You've done the job before, just get it done and have it ON my desk in the morning." The Authority does his best. The job is on the Generalist desk in the morning, and the first question the Generalist asks is, "Why did you do it this way?" No matter what the Specialist does, without the "how," his life can be challenging.

Motivation Self-Assessment

Based on what I've read in this chapter, I feel that my motivational needs are most like:

Trailblazer _____   Go-Getter _____   Manager _____   Motivator _____

Authority _____   Collaborator _____   Diplomat _____

I also have motivations similar to: _____

Working Style Self-Assessment

Based on what I've read in this chapter, I feel my style (including the do's and don'ts) is most like:

Trailblazer _____   Go-Getter _____   Manager _____   Motivator _____

Authority _____   Collaborator _____   Diplomat _____

I also have motivations similar to: _____

Chapter 7

— The Bottom Line —

➤ Learning about your personality (Tier I) marks the beginning of a new way of looking at and understanding yourself and others.
➤ Generalists are motivated by ego, status, sense of urgency, and independence.
➤ Specialists are motivated by stability, security, and structure.
➤ By reading about and observing the strategies of successful entrepreneurs with different personalities, you can discern what will work for you and how you might leverage that knowledge and awareness. Metrics represent Tier IV of our Performance Pyramid. It is a mission critical imperative to be able to measure our actions.
➤ We have motivational needs associated with each of the four behavioral factors: Dominance, Sociability, Relaxation, and Compliance.

CHAPTER

8

How Entrepreneurs And Wantrepreneurs Lead or Manage

ENTREPRENEURS ARE RARELY SATISFIED WITH EITHER THEIR PERFORMANCE OR THE performance of others. (See Figure 8.1.) On a survey question about business challenges, most respondents think they are better leaders than they are managers. In other words, they're saying it's easier to handle the strategic or leadership side of the business than the management or tactical side. The challenge is that almost every business, especially start-ups, requires more day-to-day management than leadership. Initially, the entrepreneur spends more time working *in* the business than *on* the business. An exception to this might be a well-funded launch where the entrepreneur is the visionary and has surrounded himself with those who will handle the implementation and the day-to-day operations.

FIGURE 8.1: **Surprise Business Challenges**

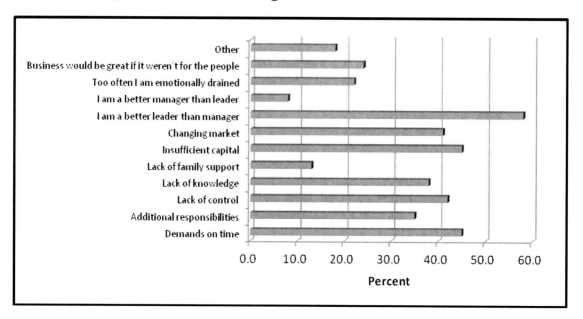

Respondents also mentioned the constraints of capitalization, lack of control, and demands on one's time. Interestingly enough, lack of control is really a behavioral issue in that most Generalist personalities rarely feel they have enough control, which makes sense for a controlling personality. Specialists, on the other hand, have an equally difficult time letting go of the details. The Generalist has a need to control the "authority," and the Specialist has a need to control the details.

The People Factors

"Selecting the right people" is the number-one challenge of the entrepreneur followed by "developing leadership capabilities" and "tapping the thinking power and creativity of your people." Managing people is difficult at best. Leading them can be overwhelming for the faint of heart. That's why it becomes so important to understand your employees, your partners, and even your significant other.

The greatest concern the entrepreneur has is selecting the right people. The Generalists have difficulty hiring strong personalities because they often have trouble working with types that are a lot like themselves. They also have a higher level of sociability, which means they tend to be internal optimists and believe the best about everyone.

FIGURE 8.2: **Top Three People Challenges**

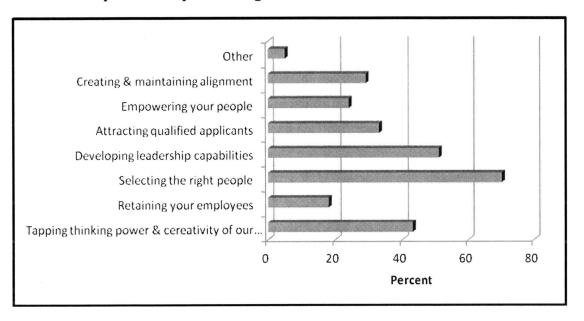

Specialists have a hard time hiring the right people because they have a tendency to only want to hire other Specialists, or people they know will do it right. Therefore, they have tremendous difficulty hiring for sales or management positions. Entrepreneurs realize that they rarely have a sustainable advantage through technology and they rarely have more money than their competition. The only competitive advantage they can sustain is achieved by having the best people in the right positions. This knowledge can make their quest to hire and retain the right people even more frustrating. For this reason they are more prone to embrace systems.

Developing leadership capabilities is difficult for Generalists because they function as if everyone is like them. One of their greatest difficulties is developing an appreciation for the differences between themselves and their staffs. They are ultimately quite short with their employees, which may get them the results they want short-term, but long-term will lead to frustrated employees and possibly high turnover. Generalists have difficulty with the introverts because they never know where they stand. They have difficulty with extroverts because they believe the extroverts are always lying or trying to sway them with emotional arguments.

Specialists have difficulty developing leadership capabilities because they always want to make sure that what they're doing is right. Their fall-back position will tend to be more education, rather than learning more leadership skills.

Tapping the thinking power and creativity of employees can be challenging for Generalists because they tend to go with their own ideas; sometimes they don't even think about enlisting the thoughts of their team. For Specialists it can be challenging because asking for employees' ideas can be like opening a can of worms.

Unlike most human resource organizations that are bound by their legal departments and therefore unwilling to take a risk, the entrepreneurs will do almost anything they can to maximize their business edge and advantage. That's why so many of them embrace the concept of hiring and managing others based on personality surveys and skills testing. They are doing what many larger companies wish they could do, and have been since way before they became popular.

The leaders surveyed were more than willing to use tools, technology, and systems to evaluate personnel.

Skills testing	31.6%
Personality testing	51.6
Intelligence testing	5.3
Background checking	47.4
360-degree assessments	9.5
Reference checks	78.9
Creativity models	5.3
Emotional Intelligence Testing	6.3
Exit interview	66.3
Other	10.5

Personality testing was the number-one response outside of the normal Human Resources (HR) focus of reference checks and exit interviews. Of those surveyed, 51.6 percent used personality testing. This is *three times greater* than in most larger businesses within the United States. Obviously, the entrepreneur is more willing to use technological accelerators in order to maintain or achieve a competitive edge.

Rarely do we meet a business owner who is satisfied with either himself or his managers. In response to questions of leadership effectiveness, entrepreneurs only gave a three on a scale of one-to-five when asked to rate the effectiveness of leaders in their organizations. And very few of the entrepreneurs gave their managers a five. As I mentioned before, business owners have a hard time understanding why others can't do what they so easily accomplish. If I don't think I'm a five, how can I give a five to others?

FIGURE 8.3: **Effectiveness of Leaders in Your Organization**

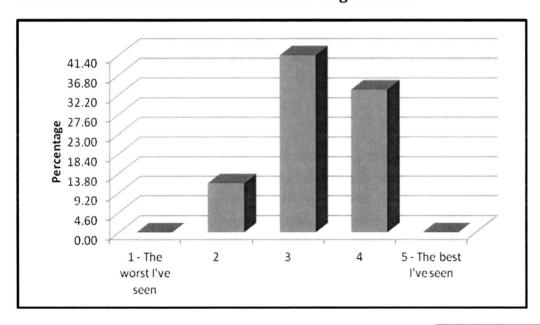

In a 1985 article in the *Harvard Business Review*, Peter Drucker said, "At most, one-third of our hires turnout right, one-third ends up mediocre at best, and one-third are outright failures. In no other area of our business would we put up with such miserable performance."

This study group indicated that only 28 percent of their employees were truly exceptional performers. Among the rest, mediocre employees are more of a concern than the poor ones. The poor ones leave or should be asked to, but the mediocre ones stay, become bitter, and can sabotage companies. During my presentations,

> **Managing People**
>
> Future leaders are offered very few college classes that prepare them for managing the people side of business. In fact, unless one is in an MBA program (with an HR bias) it is fair to say they would have very little, if any, class work that helps them learn to understand and manage the people side of business.

I've asked the following question of CEOs thousands of times: *What percentage of your employees are truly awesome performers?*

Effective Employees	CEOs
0 to 20%	29%
21 to 40%	36%
41 to 60%	24%
61 to 80%	8%
81 to 100%	3%

The answer given most often is between 20 and 25 percent. When we ask the same question of human resource managers in the same companies, the answer is closer to 60 percent. Both are right based on their perspective – it's just that the entrepreneurs are looking for more from people.

Growing Leadership Skills

"Like parenthood, leadership will never be an exact science. But neither should it be a complete mystery to those who practice it. In recent years, research has helped parents understand the genetic, psychological, and behavioral components that affect their job performance (parenting). With new research, leaders too have obtained a clearer picture of what it takes to lead effectively. And perhaps as important, they see how they can make it happen.

The business environment is continually changing, and a leader must respond in kind. Hour to hour, day to day, week to week, executives must play their leadership styles like a pro – using the right one at just the right time and in just the right measure. The payoff is in the results."

 – Excerpt from *Leadership that Gets Results*, by Daniel Coleman, in the *Harvard Business Review*.

"A leader is best when people barely know that he exists, not so good when people obey and acclaim him, worst when they despise him. Fail to honor people, they fail to honor you; but if a good leader who talks little when his work is done, his aim fulfilled, they will all say 'we did it ourselves.'"

-Lao-Tzu

"One of the greatest challenges we as leaders have is we have very little appreciation as to why others can't do what we so easily accomplish."

-Bill Wagner

Entrepreneurial inspiration could almost be an oxymoron. It's an interesting

---

The Necessary Evils in Being a Butthead

A client came to us and lamented that his company was suffering from low morale. His employees thought he was overbearing, a micromanager, and controlling. The rumor was that the employees considered the CEO to be a "butthead." The CEO was beside himself because he provided great benefits and flexibility, and legitimately cared about his employees and their well being. My company asked his employees to complete a McQuaig Job Survey, which is a tool we use to determine Tier II behavioral requirements for the CEO's position. The survey results, almost without exception, were identical to the CEO's real personality (Tier I). At this moment, the employees had an immediate shift in their thinking. They understood that the things they didn't like about the CEO were "necessary evils" in order for the CEO to deliver the goods. Their CEO was no longer an ordinary butthead but was now "their butthead." And it was because of his difficult nature that they were part of a very successful company and had their complete benefit package, 401K, stability, and tremendous security.

---

concept, however, when looking at entrepreneurs as purists. They inspire by their own doggedly determined level of tenacity. Most employees know that if they attach themselves to these rising stars, they too may have a phenomenal ride. Employees are inspired by the vision of the entrepreneur – the big-picture attitude, the ability to look and see beyond. With the exception of the entrepreneur's executive team, employees most often have the opposite personality. It's almost like a moth being attracted to a flame. The challenge is for the employees to deal with the entrepreneur's ability to create constant chaos. Entrepreneurs rarely understand their employees, and their employees rarely understand their bosses.

One of the greatest things about the entrepreneur is the tendency to be innovative, as well as creative and imaginative. Being creative is producing original thought, whereas innovation is turning original thought into something different, greater, or better.

Creative people are inspired and they often inspire others. If they are more introverted, then motivating others may be difficult. This is where entrepreneurs can fall short, especially those who aren't gifted with high levels of empathy. To them, dealing with people may not be either natural or enjoyable. A Trailblazer or Manager's idea of motivation might be lacking when viewed through the perspective of one of the more sociable personality types. For example, when an employee asks how he or she is doing, a Trailblazer or Manager might reply, "You got a paycheck, didn't you?" I hope you realize I'm taking a bit of literary license, but the personality types with low sociability can be on the terse side.

One of the greatest challenges for an entrepreneur is having an appreciation as to why others can't do what he can so easily accomplish. This is a major thought, so let me repeat it: One of the greatest challenges leaders have is they have very little appreciation as to why others can't do what they so easily accomplish. "My greatest challenge is myself," a successful entrepreneur told me. "Unfortunately, not many of the people that I do business with perform at my level. It is very difficult to sit back and watch them make mistakes."

> **Creator vs. Innovator**
>
> Thomas Edison was the creator of basic light bulb technology. Those who followed him were the innovators. I am not the first person to write about personality. I am one of a few that sees it as a model of predictability and strategic understanding and as a tool for succession.

This is the root cause of many an entrepreneur's impatience and challenging demeanor: Why did you do it that way? Why didn't you make that sale? Why can't you work that extra ten hours this week and get it done? Why can't you work overtime? Why did you take "no" for an answer? If other people could do the things entrepreneurs accomplish so easily, they wouldn't be the employees – they'd be the competition. On the other hand, how long could entrepreneurs do some of the jobs done by others in their companies? How long could entrepreneurs handle the details or work at a slow, repetitive task? Not very long, indeed.

My first real paying job was when I was 16 years old. My father got me a job sorting bottles at a Coca-Cola® bottling plant in Peoria, Illinois. In the old days people actually returned their empty bottles to the grocery store to get the deposits refunded. I thought this was a pretty great job. I got to drive the family Chevrolet Impala, I got to wear a yellow hard hat, and I got to drink all of the ice cold Coca-Cola® that I could drink all day long. I was working with three other bottle sorters who also thought this was the greatest job in the world. One had been sorting bottles for 15 years, one for 12 years, and one for eight years. On my third day at work, we ran out of bottles. The forklift driver got tied up elsewhere in the plant. When we ran out of bottles, it was like a free break. Once they delivered more bottles, I found that I was sorting bottles faster than ever. My motivation was that we would again run out of bottles, and I would get another unplanned break. As I was in my sorting frenzy, these three men looked at me and said, almost in unison, "Hey college boy – slow down – we ain't gonna run outta bottles." I thought running out of bottles was a good thing. They saw running out of bottles as a bad thing because it affected their job security. Lesson learned...to be a great leader one must either have or develop an appreciation as to the motivations of others. I wanted my independence, and the others wanted stability and security.

Can you think of a time or two when you got it wrong? In light of the fact that many of you have a spouse with the exact opposite personality, how often do you get it wrong in that environment?

Many entrepreneurs have a "telling" style of communication that stems from their technical orientation, or from a high level of dominance and a low level of sociability. Unfortunately, a telling style of communication isn't limited to those with high levels of dominance. Trailblazers, Managers, and Authorities usually all have a strong directive style of communication.

> **Delegation of Authority and Details**
>
> There are two main aspects of delegation: delegation of authority and delegation of details. Authority is the legal right to say *yes* or *no*. With that comes responsibility, and with responsibility comes the task of getting the job done. The second area of delegation is the delegation of details, e.g. giving someone a task to complete.

The challenge for the entrepreneur who has a dominant style of management is to avoid creating an organization of highly compliant "yes" people. This is a natural tendency. What he needs is an organization of leaders, people like him, an organization of self-confident employees who are willing to fight for their authority and autonomy. The Generalist has a tendency to hire Specialists, and Specialists also have a tendency to hire Specialists. Hiring is mostly a counter-intuitive process.

I discuss this further in Chapter 13, The Goldilocks Theory: Creating an Organization that Is Just Right. Also, check the resources available at www.accordmanagementsystems.com.

The more sociable entrepreneurs are challenged because they delegate authority too freely. At times they have more of a need to be liked than to deliver results. Not only do they tend to over-delegate, but they often don't follow up as closely as they should. This over-delegation can lead to loss of control and accountability. Do you see yourself in either of these examples?

The difficulty for entrepreneurs with a high level of dominance, especially those who aren't gifted with an equally high level of sociability, is that they're overly controlling. They control not only themselves, but also everyone and everything around them. They have difficulty delegating real authority and this becomes the entrepreneur's trap.

The entrepreneur's trap is the inability to delegate authority or give up control. This may limit entrepreneurs to a family or lifestyle business, as opposed to a larger, scalable business. While there is nothing wrong with a family or lifestyle business, it can limit the ultimate goals of the owner.

The real authority that highly dominant entrepreneurs delegate is usually only given to those they know and trust. Even then, they follow up excruciatingly closely and demand both metrics and results. If they don't get the results they're looking for, they can be downright nasty. And, once they've lost trust in others, it can take a long time to regain their trust. On the other hand, they can delegate responsibility when necessary or required.

With the exception of recessionary years, American business spends close to $50 billion annually purchasing information systems and technology. At the same time, only a tenth of that amount was invested in the training and development of employees. With objective systems, people know exactly what to expect. Therefore, it is essential that they adopt more objective measures for measuring both employees and their positions. These measures are extremely valuable because they allow people to better predict desired outcomes. It comes down to the old axiom: If you can't measure it, you can't manage it.

CEOs are prepared more for their jobs behaviorally than in terms of their skill sets. They see the world differently, not because they want to, but because it comes naturally. No one wakes up in the morning and decides they want to become a CEO, CIO, EIEIO, or an entrepreneur. It just happens. And, it happens because they can't stand the person they're working for, or they get fired, or they believe they're good and smart enough to take that risk. And, typically, one or two people entered our lives and made very dramatic changes or provided us with the experience, knowledge, or mentorship to prepare us for our leadership positions.

How Specific Personality Styles Lead

Have you noticed that not only do we look different from one another, but we also behave much differently? That's because we're hard-wired differently. When it comes to leadership, the chasm becomes even greater because you're not only dealing with the differences between personalities, you're also dealing with different skills, education levels, experience, and learned styles.

This section paints a picture of how each of the seven personality styles, four Generalist and three Specialist, lead and manage.

The Generalist personality is usually managing from 30,000 feet, which is great if they have organizations that are large enough that other strategic employees are in charge of execution. Where the entrepreneur struggles is handling *both* the strategy and the execution. Their difficulty is delegating and letting go of authority because they know that very few people will have a vision similar to theirs.

The Specialist personality on the other hand, has almost the exact opposite issue. Their challenge isn't delegating authority; it's delegating the details because they know that no one will do the job as well as they will.

Remember, in this segment you can gain an understanding of your employees' strengths and weaknesses as well as your own.

Trailblazers' Leadership Style

Because they have high levels of dominance and low levels of sociability, they're analytical, driven, and fairly independent. As leaders, Trailblazers have the following behaviors:

- Depending on their level of dominance, they can be highly self-assured and decisive. Not only do they expect to be the ones who make the key decisions, but also they're most comfortable in that position – comfortable making the difficult and even unpopular decisions.
- They see themselves as resourceful problem solvers and believe that decisions should be based on facts, logical thinking, and impartial analysis.

- They think the best changes are those balanced by a respect for existing systems and processes. In other words, they don't feel a need to reinvent the wheel.
- They're usually creative, imaginative, and innovative. They often come up with original ideas, and they also have the ability to take other people's ideas to the next level. This can be frustrating for others, as the Trailblazers always seem to be a step ahead. They don't always talk about their ideas, but their actions show what they're thinking.

Because they have high levels of self-confidence, they're prone to taking calculated risks; they believe they can make things happen. They have a need for change and are comfortable with it. They use their drive to maintain momentum and are careful to avoid letting emotions get in their way.

Potential Limitations

Their strong egos and aggressive natures can be intimidating, inhibiting input from others. They can easily give the impression that their minds are made up, therefore negating the need even to ask for opinions. They can be seen as setting unrealistic goals, which can instill a crisis mentality in their staffs and increase the risk of burn-out.

They focus more on facts than on people. They aren't prone to being swayed by emotional argument and, therefore, find managing sales or customer-service people a real challenge. Because of their matter-of-fact style of communication, they can come across as rude, even abrasive, especially when under pressure. They don't necessarily recognize the need to provide positive feedback, giving staff members the impression that their work is unappreciated. They've been known to intimidate employees with their sparse style of communication.

Go-Getters' Leadership Style

They have a high level of dominance, their sociability is high but still less than their dominance, and they are highly driven and independent. Go-Getters are risk-takers who not only make things happen, but make them happen fast. They embrace fast-paced environments and opportunities for change. They use their innate sense of urgency to maintain momentum and are comfortable putting pressure on both themselves and others. They're innovative in their approach and have a "Clintonesque" quality, a strong sense of empathy, and typically a high level of emotional intelligence that gives them the ability to read people. They can be optimists who sell their positive viewpoint to others, and they're good at addressing the needs and concerns of others.

This profile is typical of people who are highly results-oriented, assertive and come to work for one reason: to push for a win. Having a strong leadership style, they demonstrate the characteristics required to deal with challenging situations. Being people-oriented, they use their sociability to mitigate their potential edge.

They adopt an unstructured approach to getting things done, are comfortable with delegating the details, and are willing to look for alternative ideas. They're energetic and hard-driving, respond quickly, and cultivate a fast-paced, change-oriented workplace. Naturally outgoing and persuasive, they are able to build consensus and collaborate with others.

Self-assured and decisive, they expect to make the key decisions, seeing themselves as resourceful and influential problem solvers who focus on the big picture. They enjoy seeking out inventive solutions and firmly believe in their convictions, so they tend to make most decisions fearlessly. They put pressure on themselves and others to respond quickly, sensing a finite window of opportunity for action.

They're comfortable relying on their intuitive abilities and believe that the best decisions take the people factor into account.

Potential Limitations

Their strong confidence, ego, and aggressive, challenging nature can intimidate others and dissuade them from offering input. Unlike Trailblazers, Go-Getters rarely come across as rude, but they can be seen as way too intense. They try to control their environment and can set unrealistic goals. They can appear to have a vested interest in their own solutions and to be unreceptive to suggestions. Given their natural dislike for administrative concerns, problems can occur during the implementation phase of their initiatives because it lacks a clear and specific plan of action. Go-Getters can delegate too many of the details, leaving projects open to ultimate failure. Their lack of patience and need for immediate resolution can lead to hasty decisions and result in their putting too much pressure on their team. Go-Getters are leaders who are good at dealing with pressure and multi-tasking, but they can also have a strong tendency to procrastinate. Their need for rapid change can lead them to overlook the long-term ramifications of their initiatives. They are 30,000-foot thinkers who can find implementation to be their challenge.

Their empathy and concern for others can make it difficult for them to hold others accountable, and they sometimes place a higher value on being liked than on getting results.

Managers' Leadership Style

CDE (Career Development Elsewhere)

There is a new certification program available for those who need to be fired. It's called a CDE, for Career Development Elsewhere. (Okay, I could be more sensitive.) No, actually, I suggest two questions and two thoughts of my clients to get them to determine when it's time to fire someone:

1. If the employee you have issues with were to come into your office tomorrow to submit his resignation, and you knew of someone even better to replace him with, would you accept his resignation or try to persuade him to stay? If you're willing to accept his resignation, then perhaps it's time to let him go.
2. Think about the person that you have issues with and imagine that you are now writing him a weekly check from your own account. Would you be willing to write the employee a check from your own checking account, instead of using the business account? If not, then why are you willing to pay him with someone else's money?
3. It is said that when you first think about firing someone, that is the time to do it.
4. I once heard a CEO lament that he looked at hiring as three words: hope, faith and charity. When you first hire someone you hope they can do the job. After a couple of weeks of poor performance we have the faith they can change and later it becomes a charitable event.

Managers have a high level of dominance and a low level of sociability. They also have a high level of relaxation and are more independent than compliant. They're risk-takers who believe they can make things happen. They have a "ready, aim, aim, aim, fire" style of leadership – as opposed to the Go-Getter style which has been described as "fire, ready, aim." Their high level of relaxation makes them patient, relaxed, methodical, and calm, whereas Go-Getters and Trailblazers are much more driven, working at a faster pace. Managers' patience is also such that they're comfortable with the status quo and don't change things for the sake of changing. If it ain't broke, don't fix it. They'll want to review the alternatives before making a change, and given their analytical nature, they're equally careful not to be swayed by emotional argument.

Managers are more systems-oriented than people-oriented, but can force themselves to deal with and lead others. They're much more comfortable managing by the numbers and metrics than by having long, drawn-out conversations. What this means is that direct reports need to accomplish specific goals on a daily, weekly, or monthly basis, and employees are being held accountable to these numbers. When you hit your numbers, you get to keep your job; when you don't hit your numbers, then you are the first to know. They can adopt an unstructured approach to getting things done and can be comfortable with delegating the details. They provide practical, matter-of-fact, focused solutions and can be demanding of others. They don't enjoy emergencies or firefighting because they prefer a more long-term approach to decision making. Knee-jerk decisions are definitely not their style.

Potential Limitations

Managers' aggressive nature, which can be intimidating, is their primary limitation. Their approach limits communication, and their demanding nature can come across as rudeness. They aren't rude. They're just matter-of-fact, strictly business. Their preferred method of communication is usually e-mail or voice mail, which reinforces the reclusive perception others have of them.

Their high level of relaxation presents another challenge because it often manifests itself as stubbornness. Managers are typically very loyal individuals, often viewing their employees as an extension of the family. But this loyalty can also lead to the difficulty they experience in firing employees. As a result, Managers keep people on long after they've served their purpose. Their inability to act quickly may sometimes cause them to lose an opportunity.

Motivators' Leadership Style

Motivators have high levels of both dominance and sociability, but their sociability is greater than their dominance. They're also driven and somewhat independent. Their high level of drive gives them a tremendous ability to work well under pressure but, more importantly, they're able to put a lot of pressure on others. They move quickly, think quickly, and act or react quickly. Motivators are real people, and their high level of sociability gives them, in turn, a high level of empathy. They read people well and have a clearly defined leadership style that invites participation. Strong consensus-builders, they actually care about and often solicit the opinions of others.

Because of their belief in others, they're willing to let go and delegate authority. They are equally good at delegating the details. They can have a fairly loosely structured leadership approach to getting things done and they have the ability to collaborate. Being an agent of change, Motivators embrace it. They're great at selling their ideas and can create a strong emotional argument in order to get their way.

Potential Limitations

Their main limitations ultimately stem from their strengths. Because of their style of delegation, they can find it difficult to hold others accountable and follow up closely with them. And because of their desire to be liked, Motivators may find it difficult dealing with challenging employees. They may want to be liked at the expense of getting results. They can also have a hard time keeping their relationships with employees professional and will therefore want to avoid making unpopular decisions. Motivators are fortunate in that they have a high level of dominance that provides them with self-confidence, but with their high level of sociability, they can easily be swayed or influenced. Numbers may not be their friend, and dealing with the operational side could be equally challenging.

Motivators are often heavily involved with the sales or customer-service side of the business. They enjoy being with and working with others so much that they may avoid being alone. They need a fairly constant level of social stimulation, which puts them in a position of being taken advantage of. Another challenge is they may not be the best listeners.

Authorities' Leadership Style

Authorities have a Specialist personality in that they prefer doing things one way, the right way. They're risk-adverse and seek to have a high level of expertise. From a personality perspective, they have a high level of compliance, which is where their adversity to risk comes from. Authorities have a high level of relaxation, which is their source of stability and loyalty. They're analytical, accommodating, agreeable, and cooperative.

As leaders, they lead by example and focus on output, seeking consensus and delegating authority. They do, however, have difficulty delegating the details. Authorities are the true experts and lead based on the rules. Organized and systematic, they take a disciplined approach to leadership. They usually manage based on numbers, metrics, and expectations. They're better able to hold others accountable if they can accurately measure their performance. Authorities are careful not to overact and have a steady methodical approach. They focus more on the practical, work-oriented side of the business than on the people side.

They seek authorization, approval, and a sign-off from others before they take a risk. They're good troubleshooters and problem solvers, having a strong analytical nature. Typically good with details and numbers, authorities are often well-served when working in the backend of the business. Rarely the founders of a business, they're more comfortable buying an ongoing business.

They aren't known as agents of change because they think things through thoroughly and seek others' expertise before making decisions. The decisions they make are weighed carefully and analytically, they are composed of detail, and designed to avoid as much risk as possible.

Potential Limitations

Authorities have a need to avoid confrontation and may have difficulty being assertive and taking a proactive approach to change and accountability. They may also have a tendency to put off important decisions because they will rarely think they have enough information to make the right decision.

Their focus on details can hobble their decision-making, and their lack of big-picture perspective can lead them to analyze situations so long that they lose what little edge or initiative they had. They may have great difficulty demonstrating the determination or initiative necessary in many entrepreneurial endeavors. Like Managers, Authorities have high levels of relaxation, and the resulting loyalty is both an asset and an obstacle, making it difficult to deal with poor performers. Because of their analytical natures, it could also be difficult for Authorities to really motivate their employees.

Collaborators' Leadership Style

The main difference between the Authority profile and the Collaborator profile is that the latter has a higher level of sociability. This allows Collaborators to build stronger teams and work by, with and through others. They have accommodating, agreeable natures and high levels of relaxation and compliance.

As leaders, Collaborators assume the role of supportive team leaders, focusing on the team and discouraging internal competition among their staff members. They see their role as one of providing guidance rather than being authoritative or confrontational. They can be confrontational on occasion, but this usually occurs when someone isn't following the rules, policies or procedures. They take it and take it and take it, and when they finally explode no one knows where it comes from. Because Collaborators are so sociable, they are typically challenged by dealing with difficult people or situations. ***This challenge also surfaces when dealing with confrontation.*** To help them, my company uses a system we call "Point Easy." Point Easy is not necessarily limited to a specific personality, as everyone can benefit from being more proactive. However, it's particularly effective with Collaborators and personality types with higher sociability than dominance because it provides a means to confront issues, without being confrontational.

FIGURE 8.4: **Point Easy**

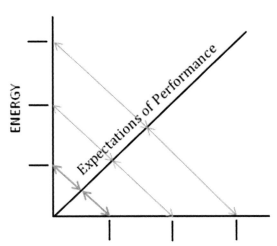

People almost always know what the expectations are for the job. The challenge takes place when the employee (or yourself, for that matter) falls away from those expectations. The only way to get back to that point is to change or confront the situation. There is a direct relationship between the amount of time it takes to coach or confront a situation and the energy that confrontation requires. Therefore, take the high road and confront the situation early in the process. It requires less energy and stress. In the long run, you'll feel better.

As leaders, Collaborators prefer to be in an environment where they have a sense of structure. Before they make decisions, they prefer having the authorization that comes from working within a well-structured environment. They rely on their intuition and their optimistic natures. As opposed to less sociable personalities, ***Collaborators are strong at building consensus in that they also ask for and value the opinions of others***.

Naturally sociable and outgoing, they try to maintain team harmony and take care of their employees. They like to think things through carefully and aren't quick to react. They want to promote a stable environment for both themselves and their organizations and work with established procedures whenever possible.

> ### The Point Easy Concept
>
> The need for Point Easy goes something like this: It is Thursday morning and one of your employees is late. You hesitate to bring this to his attention because you don't want to create an issue, ruin his morale, or have it cost you another day's worth of wages. So, you decide to mention it at the end of his shift. But, guess what? You get tied up and forget to mention it.
>
> You justify this by saying, "I'll mention it to him first thing in the morning." But, guess what? On Friday he is absent. By the time Monday rolls around, you've worried about it even though you missed your opportunity. Do you think the employee in question gave his tardiness and absence more than a moment's thought? I doubt it, but you spent hours fretting over what to do and when to do it. Use the Point Easy concept and get on with life.

There is a direct relationship between the delay in my saying something and the amount of energy it requires. Quick conversations equal less energy; delayed conversations require more energy.

They're reluctant to initiate change until they can ensure that they have the necessary support, and they do what they can to minimize disruptions and confrontation. Collaborators are comfortable selling their ideas to others in a warm safe environment. When it comes to change, they take a fairly low-key approach and always maintain a high level of sensitivity to other people and their opinions.

Potential Limitations

Collaborators will often do just about anything to avoid confrontation. Because of their high level of sociability, their optimistic natures, and their desire not to alienate or offend others, they can have difficulty holding others accountable. Our experience is that through the use of the Point Easy concept, they can hold others accountable by using a system and therefore removing themselves from the equation.

With their need to avoid conflict, they may have difficulty being assertive and providing a proactive direction. They may also have a tendency to procrastinate when faced with decisions outside their areas of expertise. In these situations, Collaborators will do what they can to develop that expertise but, until they do, their decision-making skills will degrade until they have the requisite knowledge.

Diplomats' Leadership Style

Of all the Specialists, Diplomats probably have the best service-related leadership profile. This is because they are very caring by nature and need to do things by the book. They have high levels of compliance and sociability, and low levels of dominance and relaxation, meaning that they're driven as well.

As leaders, they are typically more comfortable guiding their team and employees, as opposed to giving them orders. This selling style of communication works well in retail and customer service environments. In particular, Diplomats encourage cohesion rather than conflict or competition, especially among their staff. They respond to situations quickly and work well under pressure. They have a high sense of urgency and need to get things done quickly. They take an organized and systematic approach to administration and leading others. Because they're naturally sociable and outgoing, they make a concerted effort to maintain team commitment and are especially willing to address the needs and concerns of their employees and customers.

They prefer to lead by example and really focus on the team. They'll use their own need for speed to demonstrate their concern for getting things done quickly. Because of their drive, they'll act quickly but with a careful approach to doing the right thing. They systematically look at precedents before choosing a course of action and seem to focus on the tactics rather than on the big-picture, strategic side of the business. Generally risk-adverse, they take a safety-first approach.

Potential Limitations

Since Diplomats need to do things one way (the right way), they have difficulty dealing with ambiguity. Their desire to be liked can make it difficult for them to keep it professional, to hold others accountable, and to make difficult people decisions. They're so good at managing by consensus that they can have difficulty asserting their position. This

---

Mitigating Your Edge

The potential limitations of all personality types can be mitigated, provided they understand and embrace the right behavioral changes. Remember:

Tier I: *Personality* provides people with both their strengths and potential limitations.

Tier II: *Behaviors* provide them with the direction necessary to do their jobs and change. The change is reflected in...

Tier III: *Actions* which, when accomplished, provide us with the appropriate Tier V results.

can also manifest itself in acceptance of lower levels of performance, because of Diplomats' challenge in dealing with confrontation.

Their by-the-book natures and need to monitor their teams' activities can leave employees feeling micromanaged. Diplomats may also have difficulty dealing with widely varied and often unpredictable entrepreneurial activities. They are, therefore, best in moderately structured work environments such as a franchise or distributorship that have a retail or a strong social orientation.

Leadership Style Self-Assessment

Based on what I've read in this chapter, I feel that my leadership style is most like:

___Trailblazer
___Go-Getter
___Manager
___Motivator
___Authority
___Collaborator
___Diplomat
___I also have qualities similar to:_____

Chapter 8

— The Bottom Line —

- ➤ Entrepreneurs are rarely satisfied with either their performance or the performance of their people.
- ➤ "Selecting the right people" is the number-one challenge of the entrepreneur followed by "developing leadership capabilities" and "tapping the thinking power and creativity of your people."
- ➤ The five-tier Performance Pyramid is equally important to use with existing employees. This allows entrepreneurs to better direct their efforts, hold others accountable, and measure their results.
- ➤ The entrepreneur has the opposite personality from many of his employees.
- ➤ One of the greatest challenges business owners have is that they have very little appreciation as to why others can't do what entrepreneurs so easily accomplish. But if employees could accomplish the same things as entrepreneurs, they wouldn't be their employees; they would become their competition.
- ➤ The challenge for the entrepreneur, who has a telling style of communication, is to avoid creating an organization of highly compliant employees (yes people).
- ➤ One of the challenges of the more sociable entrepreneurs is they delegate authority– perhaps too freely.

CHAPTER

9

Knowledge Is the World's Equalizer

THERE IS A DIRECT RELATIONSHIP BETWEEN THE AMOUNT OF TIME entrepreneurs invest in their education and their long-term success. I once heard two successful entrepreneurs say, "The harder I work, the luckier I get." And the other added, "I have more good luck than my competition has bad luck." You can rest well-assured that there is definitely a relationship between how smart you work and the results you achieve.

"There are no exceptions to the rule that everybody likes to be an exception to the rule."

– Malcom Forbes

Building consensus isn't a natural act for the majority of entrepreneurs because they're more controlling and have a need to be very hands-on in their management style. Because of this, building consensus is a learned skill for most of them, and this learning comes only through hard work. The currency the entrepreneur spends in his development is the number of hours he invests in himself.

The entrepreneurs surveyed invest an average of 110 hours each year in their training, learning and development. Assuming an eight-hour workday, that amounts to a whopping 13 days, or over two weeks, each year. Knowledge is the world's equalizer and provides the greatest advantage when it comes to retaining that all-important competitive edge. Learning is one of the greatest investments in success that anyone can make.

It seems as if employees stop learning about the same time they graduate college. I've interviewed hundreds of applicants for clients in the past several years, and one of the questions I ask them is, "Can you name several of the last business books or publications you've read?" Unfortunately most applicants stopped reading when they were last in school. I also ask applicants to write a 1,000-word SWOT (Strengths, Weaknesses, Opportunities, Threats) analysis about our business. Several applicants have indicated that they weren't willing to write a 1,000-word report to get a job. If they aren't willing to invest 1,000 words to get a job, what are the chances that they'll be willing to write 1,000 words to keep a job? Not very good.

FIGURE 9.1: **Time Invested on Personal Development/Education (Annual)**

Hours	Percent
0 to 100	55%
101 to 200	21%
201 to 300	10%
301 to 400	2%
401 to 500	4%
501 to 600	2%
601 to 700	2%
701 to 800	1%
800+	3%
Source: YEO Survey	

Building Consensus

How the entrepreneur builds consensus: The Trailblazer and Manager may say, "What? I should care about someone else's opinion?" The Generalists think, "I am right." The Specialists think, "It is right."

Consensus building is the one process that must occur in order for us to get buy-in from our employees, partners, and those whom we need on our team. For about 50 percent of male entrepreneurs and 70 percent of female entrepreneurs, building consensus is part of their nature because they have a higher-than-average level of sociability. But not all entrepreneurs are concerned with building consensus. They're more likely to think, "This is what I want to do, and either you're with me or against me." Unfortunately, it's often the latter. Many entrepreneurs are so self-confident that they can't imagine seeking others for their opinions or buy-in.

Investing in Self-Development

I have been a member of Vistage since 2002. I can honestly say that I have finally become a good leader. From a Jim Collins, *Good to Great* perspective, I still have a way to go. But, I have the right Tier I: Personality...I know the right Tier II: Behaviors...and about 80 percent of the time I am able to muster the right Tier III: Actions. Between my monthly CEO meetings, my monthly one-on-ones with my coach, the educational events sponsored by the National Speakers Association and the Institute of Management Consultants, and my development coach, I easily invest 140+-hours into my own development each year. School only gets us so far; the rest we have to do ourselves.

People who are more accepting than dominant are most apt to build consensus. You can hear it in the way they talk to others. For example, they might ask, "Well, how do you feel about this?" Or, "What do you think about this?" Listen to their words. Are they concerned with how to get others on board in order to achieve agreement and eventually a goal? Have you taken care of your staff's needs? Does an inability to build consensus limit your ability to grow a company? It could and often does but, on the other hand, there are times when building consensus gets in the way of getting the results you want – when you want them. It means balancing priority and timing.

The Challenger Disaster

Remember the Space Shuttle Challenger disaster? The "I am right" administrators were under a lot of pressure from the Reagan administration to get the Challenger into space. There were months of delays. This was to be a great PR opportunity for NASA. Before a launch, each area of responsibility has to acknowledge its readiness and grant its approval. Needing its sign-off, the administrators at NASA spoke with one of the engineering groups in Utah. Its recommendation was to delay the launch because it was going to be too cold that night. Engineers explained that when they'd previously retrieved the spent external fuel tanks after other launches, they found a degradation of the "O" rings. This was believed to be related to the low ambient temperature during pre-launch. When the rings become cold during the night, they harden. When they're quickly exposed to thousands of degrees of temperature, they have a tendency to crack.

So, there were the Authority engineers being told by the Trailblazers that they wanted to get this bird in the air. The Trailblazer (the "I am right" people) were forcing the issue. The engineers (the "It is right" people) were saying, "We don't recommend it." Finally, it came down to a Trailblazer's asking, "Can you tell me if we launch that we are going to have a problem?"

Obviously, the answer was "No, we can't tell you we're going to have a problem, but we don't recommend it." When push came to shove, the engineers gave in. Although they felt they were doing the wrong thing, they couldn't stand up to the "I am right" people. The rest is history.

The highly dominant entrepreneur thinks, "I am right. I know about this, and this is what I want to do." People who are more compliant are concerned with whether something is *right*, with respect to the right way to do things. The battle lines are thus drawn: "I am right. This is the way I want to do it," versus "It is right."

Many partners, of both the business and spousal variety, encounter a similar challenge in the "I am right" versus "It is right" conflict. In business, they battle until the partnership dissolves, and the "It is right" Specialist is often left with the business. Meanwhile, the "I am right" entrepreneur goes off to start another business. The "I am right" guys are the ones who make it all happen and are usually the founders of new businesses. It is, however, their Specialist partners that make the backend of the business work. You will notice throughout the comment sections, the survey respondents had very few positive comments about partners. The partnerships that work best are those where both partners understand each other – really understand each other.

"Evaluate your partners as closely as you would your potential spouse," said one entrepreneur surveyed. I think you have to evaluate your potential partners even more than you do your spouse. You spend more time with your partners and, in good times, it's real easy getting along. In bad times, they can create the worst of times.

Another battleground exists between the extroverts and introverts. Generally those in finance, accounting, and the legal department are more introverted; their extrovert opposites are found in sales. The extroverts are more optimistic, upbeat, and sales-oriented in their style of communication. Since introverts prefer a realistic and analytical approach, the selling style of communication can lead to a lack of trust. Introverts can't stand the thought of being swayed by emotional argument.

Finding the Friction

If friction is found within a company, typically it exists between two specific areas or departments. Of the following five areas, where do you think we see it most?

Operations
Sales
Finance
Research & Development
Human Resources

The friction takes place between sales and almost any of the other areas of the company. Have you figured out why?

Chapter 9

— The Bottom Line —

➢ Entrepreneurs are rarely satisfied with either their performance or the performance of their people.
➢ "Selecting the right people" is the number-one challenge of the entrepreneur followed by "developing leadership capabilities" and "tapping the thinking power and creativity of your people."
➢ The five-tier Performance Pyramid is equally important to use with existing employees. This allows entrepreneurs to better direct their efforts, hold others accountable, and measure their results.
➢ The entrepreneur has the opposite personality from many of his employees.
➢ One of the greatest challenges business owners have is that they have very little appreciation as to why others can't do what entrepreneurs so easily accomplish. But if employees could accomplish the same things as entrepreneurs, they wouldn't be their employees; they would become their competition.
➢ The challenge for the entrepreneur, who has a telling style of communication, is to avoid creating an organization of highly compliant employees (yes people).
➢ One of the challenges of the more sociable entrepreneurs is they delegate authority– perhaps too freely.

CHAPTER

10

How Entrepreneurs and Wantrepreneurs Sell

THERE'S A VERY STARK DIFFERENCE BETWEEN SALES AND MARKETING. Salespeople get paid for their results, and marketing people get paid for their efforts. That really just about sums it up. I could be more erudite and say selling is more tactical and marketing is more strategic, but the truth is that nothing happens until someone makes a sale and the CEO needs to be the company's best salesperson.

Right before our daughter Rebecca's last birthday, she received a catalog in the mail displaying all the latest electronics: iPads®, smart phones, various handheld devices. It had just what every college student wants. What took place next was marvelous. Rebecca looked at the catalog, then looked at her mother, and said, "Mom, you said I should get a new electronic tablet for my birthday. Which would you say is best?" So, I'm thinking, "You go girl – an assumptive close and a choice close all in one question." My wife looked at me and asked, "What are you teaching the children?" I said, "Survival skills."

Those of us who consider sales to be an art form *and* a profession know what the following terms mean: choice close, assumptive close, warm market, cold market, and reduce it to the ridiculous. The average close doesn't take place until you ask for the order more than five times, and the average salesperson stops after the first or second "no."

Sales Terms/Insider Jargon

- *Choice close.* Do you want the red car or the white car?
- *Assumptive close.* Mom, didn't you tell me I should get a new car?
- *Warm market.* The market created when people respond to a mailing, a phone call or a visit to your store, location or web site. (They are just one step away from being a friend.)
- *Cold market.* Those you don't know. For example, a telemarketer dialing for dollars every day.
- *Reduce it to the ridiculous.* When you buy our program for one year, the cost per day is only a dime.
- *Selling cycle.* The typical length of time it takes to go from an introduction to closing the sale.
- *Professional visitor.* A salesperson that is unable to ask for the business for fear of ruining the relationship.
- *Professional closer.* A salesperson that is able to ask for the order until he receives it.
- *Trial close.* The salesperson asks, "If I could get this product for you at that price, would you then be willing to proceed?"
- *Transactional sale.* When you sell based on a single transaction or a single event.
- *Relationship sale.* When you sell based on the relationships you've developed.

A past article on salespeople, which ran in Harvard Business Review, professes that you can invest in all the training in the world, but if you're training the wrong people, you won't get the right results. This *really* is a critical point.

Therefore, part of the challenge regarding people is the fact that, while everyone needs to sell, each personality type goes about it differently, some more effectively and some less. As you read the following descriptions of how each personality type sells, give some thought to what your style is and what you can do to improve it to grow yourself and your business.

The sales process is three-pronged:

1. Prospecting and closing business
2. Delivery
3. Administrivia (Excuse me, Administration)

Depending on the type of sale, salespeople should spend about 70 percent of their time prospecting and closing business, 20 percent on delivery of their products or services, and the remaining 10 percent on administration. Fortunately or unfortunately, it is your personality that determines where you spend your time and with what ease. If you have a Go-Getter or Trailblazer personality, for example, you will prefer spending your time prospecting and growing the business. Mangers and Diplomats would rather handle the delivery. Motivators, Collaborators, and Diplomats enjoy the delivery and the Authorities and Managers enjoy the administrivia.

Consider Tom Cruise in the movie, *Jerry Maguire*. Was Jerry a closer, or was he more of a professional visitor? Have you thought about it? If not, think about it. If you thought he was a closer, perhaps your rationale is the fact that he exhibited a very high level of energy and was aggressively moving all over the place. But, when you look at the other side of his frenetic approach, did it really land him a client? It didn't. Throughout the entire movie, one prospect after another was closed by someone else. He had no clients and was down to one prospect. If he didn't sign Rod Tidwell, he'd be out of business. He had one shot. He was standing outside Tidwell's home in the Arizona desert. He bent over, covered his face with his hands, took a deep breath, and as he raised his head, he slightly raised his arms from his side, indicating a moment of triumph. He was ready, he was jazzed, he was changing his behaviors, and the rest is history. What was Jerry doing? To be more technical, as well as precise, Jerry knew the Tier II: Behaviors that were necessary and he was able to manifest the right Tier III: Actions in order to get the right Tier IV: Metrics. "Show me the money," and lastly...the Tier V: Results equaled a new client. As you read about the various personalities, see whether you can tell which type most fits Jerry. And, see if you can determine whether he is a closer or a professional visitor. (The answers are at the end of this chapter.)

Trailblazers' Selling Style

Trailblazers have a high level of dominance and are analytical, driven, and relatively independent. Despite their dominance, they sometimes lack the sociability that can be so valuable in selling or building relationships.

Many Trailblazers lack a strong people approach. However, they *do* share the other three characteristics found in many aggressive closers, specifically dominance, drive, and independence. They love the challenge of opening new businesses and closing new accounts, but aren't so enamored with account maintenance (convincing a client to invest additional amounts in their products or services, or up-selling).

Taking a direct approach, they concentrate on the measurable benefits of the sale itself and therefore favor a more transactional sale where the relationship is secondary. Given a choice, they'd much rather deal in the factual, objective side of selling.

Because of their high level of drive, they aren't gifted with a high level of patience. This puts them in a position where they want to close often and quickly. This is just as well because they can easily get bored with a long-term selling cycle. They're more detail-oriented and controlling than most salespeople, prepare carefully for their calls, and taking an organized approach to selling. Thanks to their high level of dominance, they need to control the sales process, and they get downright cranky if they can't.

When it comes to prospecting, they can be very competitive and direct, using all their capabilities. Because of this, they aren't necessarily the best listeners. Being objective, they don't take rejection or resistance personally; they just figure they have to get through hearing "no" five times before they're going to hear a "yes." Rapport can be a four-letter word for them because it can slow down the process and get in the way of business.

Many Trailblazers have a unique talent, which I believe stems from their motivational or manipulative gene. (Not really, but this talent does appear to be innate!) They can use others as a vehicle to get their jobs accomplished, typically without the others even knowing that is what's happening. A Trailblazer will call and invite you over to watch the game and get you to stop at the store and pick up the food and drinks. If he's really good, he can even get you to pay for them.

Trailblazers look at selling as if it's a game of mental chess. They keep their eyes on the prize and are constantly looking for another way to close the business. Given that their presentations are so objective, their manner is often mistaken for a lack of sensitivity to the feelings of others. They can also miss many of these important selling clues. Another challenge for Trailblazers is getting motivated to make the sales pitch. They often need more time to prepare or they need more data.

When it comes to closing, they're exceptionally success-oriented and aggressive. Their analytical nature allows them to focus more on the facts, figures, data, and analysis. Another one of the Trailblazer's challenges is his intensity and drive: He doesn't want to sit around and wait for someone to make a decision.

Go-Getters' Selling Style

Go-Getters are often considered the consummate closers or salespeople. They have high levels of both dominance and sociability, and since the dominance is higher, they are results-oriented. Their high sociability gives them a great sense about people, their needs, wants, and desires. But, they're more interested in the close. They're also highly driven and independent, two more factors that can strengthen their sales abilities.

Go-Getters are well-suited for generating business, especially in new or tough markets. They're aggressive and can sometimes be considered too aggressive. They live for the challenge of finding new markets and opening new accounts. Because this is more fun and rewarding for them than maintaining existing relationships, they can neglect or even ignore the maintenance part of their business. When they communicate with existing clients, their intentions have more to do with up-selling than just visiting and chatting

> ### Path-of-Least-Resistance Marketing
>
> In a previous life, I worked for Cheshire, (a Xerox Company) in Phoenix. I was selling a small binder that made a perfect bind, a product designed for the legal profession. I looked at the market and realized I could either begin calling on law firms one at a time or find a better way to reach the market. Marketing individually seemed too tedious, so I bound about 100 samples, used a photo of an attractive model clad in underwear (briefs) on the cover page, and placed a caption that read, "Do your briefs get in a bind? If not, then perhaps we should be binding your briefs." I received a ton of phone inquiries, sold a bunch of equipment, and quickly became Cheshire's top sales representative in the Western region. This is an example of what I refer to as path-of-least-resistance marketing.

with clients. Go-Getters maintain a certain attitude in that if you want their time, you will have to compensate them for it. In other words, buy something.

They can be innovative in their methods and manner of selling if it brings them closer to the ultimate goal: the close. They deal well with pressure and can work on a wide range of projects at the same time. But they also can be distracted, lose their focus, and procrastinate. They still get it done though, and many of them work so well under pressure that they make it look easy. They can be among the best networkers because they tend to place people into two categories: people they know and people they've yet to meet. And the question foremost in their minds is, "What can I sell them?"

Their prospecting nature can best be described as extremely competitive and proactive. Rarely satisfied with what they have, they want the biggest territory and more and more opportunities. Go-Getters are very independent and always look for better or more productive ways to get to their markets.

Go-Getters have a high level of energy, which allows them to thrive on pressure, meet their quotas, and rise to the challenge of constantly prospecting. Their presentations are always goal-oriented because they set direction, maintain control, and push for results. Expect a fast-paced presentation with a number of trial closes. They're always closing, and their customers rarely realize they're being sold. Their presentations are all about the customers – not the presenter.

Go-Getters are strong closers, especially within a new business environment. They're usually good at reading body language and empathetic enough to understand the subtleties of a prospect's emotions. They use that information to build a stronger relationship, thereby minimizing the customer's anxiety. Getting up and motivated can occasionally be a challenge, as they often make excuses that they need more time to prepare or they need more data.

Suggestions for a customer: Just buy!

Managers' Selling Style

Managers have a strong level of dominance and are more autonomous than sociable. They differ from Go-Getters in that they're more analytical and relaxed. Because of this, their selling style will be much different than those previously discussed.

Lacking a strong people-oriented approach and a strong sense of urgency, this profile is not well-suited to new business development or tough markets. They're most comfortable selling in or to a technical community where their low-key approach gives them a selling advantage.

Strong-minded, they hate being told what to do, so it's fairly simple to manage or motivate them. Just give them their independence in exchange for complying with a number of rules or metrics. Their technical approach leads them to speak in a matter-of-fact, strictly business manner, which is sometimes too direct. They almost always approach their prospects with quantifiable benefits and favor business that, frankly, doesn't require relationships. Their natural selling style is transactional. They're loyal to their clients as well as their company. Because of their higher-than-average level of relaxation, they do well in a longer selling cycle and, in turn, can sometimes miss opportunities for a quick close.

When prospecting, they can be extremely competitive, always looking for opportunity. Listening may not be their forte. Those who overcome this typically do so by training themselves to repeat back what the prospect is saying or even write it down. This practice also gives Managers the opportunity to really think things through. Because of their independence, Managers have a tendency to be strong-willed even in the face of uncertainty or resistance. They don't back down easily. In some arenas that might be a drawback, but in sales it's nearly always an advantage as long as it doesn't come across as being rude or stubborn.

Because Managers are so analytical and objective in their approach, they deal well with rejection and rarely take it personally. If they do take it personally, no one will know it because they internalize their emotions. Systematic, they do a good job of maintaining their focus in a presentation. They follow a planned path and don't jump around. They do best in a prospecting environment where they can establish control and have a steady-paced approach to their prospecting activities.

When presenting, they're very goal-oriented as they set their direction, maintain control of the sales-interview process, and work their presentation to achieve their goals. Because of their strong focus, they can miss or discount dissenting signals from their prospects or customers. On the other hand, this helps them to keep asking for the sale.

They tend to be both aggressive and systematic when closing. Remember, they're doggedly determined and persistent but do things on their own good time. Although this can be an asset in a long selling cycle, it can also prevent them from putting as much pressure on the situation as may be necessary.

The Network Infrastructure Corporation is a client. Their CEO, Frank Spaeth, has a Manager's personality. He's not only a great CEO, but also a great sales representative. He has the results orientation that comes with a high level of dominance, and because of his lower sociability level, he also has the technical orientation that allows him to speak the language of his technical clients. Just don't send Frank to a networking event and expect him to enjoy himself.

Motivators' Selling Style

Motivators have high levels of both dominance and sociability, but their sociability is greater. They're also very driven and independent, meaning they think well on their feet and display a higher-than-average level of energy, wanting to move things along quickly.

They're good at generating new business, and they're also good at dealing with some of the more mundane aspects of managing existing accounts. Thriving on pressure, they push to move sales along quickly, and they prefer a shorter selling cycle. In long-term sales, they have the drive to continuously move the sale along as long as they're hitting their marks and reaching the desired milestones. For example, they may want to set a second appointment before the end of the first appointment.

They're outgoing, extroverted, and innately perceptive and persuasive. They get their way through the use of warmth and friendliness. They enjoy the networking side of business and clearly prefer building relationships to taking a just-the-facts approach.

When prospecting, they can be highly competitive, but they may not deal well with prospects who don't' take warmly to them. They can't understand why someone might not like them, and they don't handle rejection well at all. Their energetic side allows them to focus – seemingly easily – on many prospects at the same time. They have a need for constant action and movement, and it can become frustrating to them if things don't move along as quickly as they prefer. Being independent, they want to and are good at figuring things out on their own.

Their presentations are typically goal-oriented, and they are good at setting their own direction. They maintain a strong level of control in the sales-interview process. They're good at establishing a sense of urgency in the process, but almost always do so in a warm fashion. They're the consummate rapport builders and use those skills (behaviors) to nullify the potential for rejection or to avoid situations where they might be confronted adversely. They're strong believers in the tightness of their arguments, but because of their sociability, they have the ability to be flexible enough to accommodate the needs of their customers and be open to others' points of view.

Motivators are success-oriented and can show considerable strength in asking for the order. They close often and early in the process. They also grow frustrated and bored with long delays. They understand the subtleties of a prospect's emotions and do a good job of reading their needs. Generally, they're persistent in closing. One of their few challenges is that not all Motivators are great with numbers. It is therefore important for them to make numbers their friends. Because of their lack of interest in details, paperwork can present a challenge. From an entrepreneurial perspective, they're great at the people side, which means their corresponding opposite side isn't so great. It's people vs. numbers.

Authorities' Selling Style

Authorities have high levels of compliance and relaxation, as well as are analytical and accepting. This makes them want to do things right. It may also mean they find the selling process challenging. It's not unusual for Authorities to think that selling shouldn't be part of their responsibilities. It's an unproductive thought, since being in business for yourself makes selling an essential part of *your* responsibility for *your* company's success. Authorities work better when they're part of a supportive team or process, so new business development can be challenging. They're very good, however, with sales follow-up and implementation. They do well when they're able to sell in a nonassertive environment where they work with add-on sales, repeat orders, or in a warm market like a retail store or professional services.

They're very detail-oriented and thorough in their preparation, but may find it difficult to stay on track if they meet resistance. They perform better with prospects who have decided to buy but need specific help with the complexity of the purchase or those who need help with their selection. Authorities have a relaxed and analytical nature and therefore do better with a longer selling cycle and stable relationships. They also excel with the technical application of the sale because they're good at understanding the complexities of the product or service. As long as they're dealing within the bounds of their expertise, they're fine. Outside this area, it's a whole different story as they want to learn more before they are totally comfortable proceeding.

When prospecting, they're more effective either with in-bound customers or in an office or retail environment. They can prospect outside, but do better if it's based on a warm lead, like following up on telemarketing leads or responses from a mailing. They're very systematic in their approach, and because they lack a tremendous level of drive, they do best in a more stable environment. This could be route sales or distributorships where there are, by the way, a tremendous number of entrepreneurial opportunities.

Authorities' style of presentation is consultative – they provide the prospect with choices or a range of opportunities from which to select. Remember, Authorities are Specialists and can give great presentations when they're talking about their areas of expertise. They're able to deal with topics of tremendous complexity and many specifications. They maintain a strong focus on the details, which can lead them to concentrate more on the fine points than on the big picture. This is appropriate given that Specialists are better at the details than the strategy.

They almost always sell with an objective focus. They know the process of the presentation and may not be comfortable when the customer changes direction. They can deal with change – they just don't like it.

They're best at closing with a choice close or in an environment where the customer makes the buying decision. If they sense too much resistance, they may defer the sale or the close until later. They don't display a high sense of urgency, allowing the customer to dictate the speed of the sale.

Collaborators' Selling Style

Collaborators are the high-sociability version of Authorities. They're still Specialists and prefer doing things the right way, but they're more relaxed and accepting than Authorities.

They also work better in supportive roles. From an entrepreneurial perspective, they're great in retail, office, route-sales, and many franchise environments. They prefer building relationships to taking the all-business approach of those with lower levels of sociability. They have a good consultative style and shy away from the more transactional or confrontational styles of selling. They have the patience for a long selling cycle and the time it can take to build and nurture a relationship. Rome wasn't built in a day, after all, or a week, or a year.

When prospecting, Collaborators are better served by working in warm markets such as in-bound leads, especially when the prospects need more information. Taking a proactive prospecting approach goes very much against their grain. Because of their sociable nature, they do well when they can build rapport and maintain relationships just by being themselves. Averse to risk-taking, they prepare for their calls and presentations. They can fall back on their sociability if and when they get into trouble. They do well with a scripted or repetitive response, and once they've been trained properly, they maintain what they learn.

They present in a manner that uses their relationships to their benefit. They prefer a warm consultative role in presentations where they are facilitating solutions with willing buyers. They're usually open and cooperative and base their communication on empathy and respect. They present in a systematic, laidback manner and can be taken off track when they're selling to a strong Generalist who keeps interrupting and asking them to get to the bottom line.

Their closing style is to encourage a customer to make the buying decision. Collaborators will usually defer to the customer when met with resistance. Because of their sociability, they understand the subtleties of prospects' emotions and will usually focus more on their emotional needs than on the facts. Because of their patient nature, they deal well with longer selling cycles. From a management perspective, they may not always be comfortable closing and may therefore require frequent coaching and support to deal with the objections that can prevent a sale.

Diplomats' Selling Style

Diplomats have perhaps the best selling personality of all the Specialists. Like the other Specialists, they're compliant and accepting, but Diplomats also have more drive and sociability. These two factors help them to excel on the people side of the business and do so with a greater sense of urgency.

They're the royalty of retail. Actually, I should say they're the royalty of the "people" environment. In retail, distributorships, any kind of selling that involves recurring or ongoing relationships, they're your sales reps. They work well under pressure and can also put pressure on those around them, but they do it with warmth. They build consensus, collaborate with others, and are most comfortable when working with and through others. The Diplomat can be the master of the Specialist relationship builders.

They prospect best in warm markets, building business relationships with existing clients or responding to in-bound calls or customers. With the right training, motivation, and support, they can also do well when prospecting in retail-based environments or highly structured outside sales environments. Remember, they want to do things the right way. If you tell them what the right way is, they'll work toward that goal. Their restless, energetic approach spurs prospecting activity as long as they don't run into too much rejection or frustration. They prepare for their calls with a fairly high level of planning. Good at building rapport, they enjoy regular people contact and can become downright cranky if they don't have the social stimulation they require. Their risk is that they may want to be liked at the expense of getting the desired results.

When presenting to prospects, they deal well within their areas of expertise and are able to answer most questions based on their knowledge and preparation. They deliver an energetic, fast-paced presentation, imparting a sense of urgency in their message. They're open and agreeable, and this allows them to be good students and readers of others. Because they're such good communicators, they may not be the best listeners, especially with a technically-oriented prospect.

For Diplomats, closing comes more easily when it's initiated by the customer. They can have difficulty asking for the order, because they want to be liked: "If I ask for the order, I might put my relationship with the prospect at risk." They understand the emotions of others and are able to respond in an appropriate manner. They may not be natural closers, but will probably be open to coaching. Because of their drive, they do best with a shorter selling cycle.

Remember the question, "Was Jerry Maguire more of a closer or a professional visitor – and which of the seven personality types was he?

Jerry was a professional visitor and a Diplomat. Remember at the beginning of the movie when he wakes up in the middle of the night and begins writing his manifesto? His concerns are two: taking care of the people (sociability) and not treating clients as slabs of meat. This shows a high level of compliance and sociability, as he was more concerned with creating a book for guidance.

If you have high levels of sociability and compliance, you will more than likely have a lot of drive (this is where Jerry's energy came from) and be accommodating, agreeable, and cooperative. This adds up to difficulty in closing the deal, just like Jerry.

Selling Style Self-Assessment

Based on what I've read in this chapter, I feel that my selling style is most like:

___Trailblazer
___Go-Getter
___Manager
___Motivator
___Authority
___Collaborator
___Diplomat
___I also have qualities similar to: _____

Chapter 10

— The Bottom Line —

➢ If you provide the right training to the wrong people (personality) you can't expect the right results.
➢ Generalists have a tendency to be better closers when it comes to a "cold market."
➢ Generalists can also close "warm market" prospects as well.
➢ Specialists have a tendency to be better closers when it comes to a "warm market."
➢ Specialists have difficulty closing difficult prospects.
➢ We have professional closers and professional visitors… Jerry McGuire was a visitor.
➢ Your best sales representatives spend 70 percent of their time prospecting, 20 percent on delivery, and 10 percent on administrivia.
➢ It is imperative that you use a personality test to help select your sales representatives.
➢ Actually, you should use personality testing for all positions.

PART

III

Win, Lose,
or Draw

CHAPTER

11

What Makes Personalities Tick and What Ticks Them Off

MANY OF US LEARNED THE GOLDEN RULE IN SUNDAY SCHOOL – OR HEARD about it on CNN. "Do unto others as you would have them do unto you." That works great if people have similar personalities and are motivated by the same things.

What you really want to live and work by is the following: "Do unto others as they would have us do unto them." In other words, understand the motivational needs of each person you deal with. This chapter presents several ideas on what each personality type really needs to make it tick and what, if you don't honor their personalities, will tick them off.

Here is a major point... when you have employees it is essential to get the most from them and the best way to do that is to know what motivates them.

But keep in mind, the lists here are only the tip of the proverbial iceberg. Ideally, you use these lists as a starting point and are then open to suggestions. Ask your employees or team members, "What can I do to really motivate you?" "What are the things that I do that tick you off?" Get the idea? By the way, when a Trailblazer tells you what ticks them off...*Don't do it.*

Trailblazers' Code of Conduct

Very dominant and more analytical than sociable, Trailblazers are driven and independent. They are all about results. They have very few friends, but ones they have are for life. Being liked is an expense they would prefer not risking; therefore, they show up for work for one reason – to win.

Are You Open for a Suggestion?

A number of years ago I was playing Chutes and Ladders with my daughter Rebecca. She was three years old at the time. This is about the time she was learning to count and develop a forward-thinking ability. She was now able to determine what number she wanted the spinner to stop on so that she could go up the ladder. Being equally astute, she was also able to determine the number the spinner should stop on for me to go down the chute. Having determined both of these key concepts, she began stopping the game spinner so that it was in her favor. This might have been tolerable had I been winning, but I was losing and I don't enjoy losing. I know, I know, the throngs of great parents are thinking, "How could you not want your daughter to win?" Well, I hadn't taken that course yet.

I needed intervention. I called out to my wife, "I can't play with Rebecca. She's cheating." To which Renee calmly replied, "Bill, Rebecca is three. You, on the other hand, are 45 and it is inappropriate for you to tattle." Rebecca, who is now 20, is a junior at Bard College in New York. She has a Generalist personality and when she wants something from me she asks, "Dad, are you open for a suggestion?" And I listen.

The following could tick off Trailblazers:

- *Controlling their activities too closely.* Do so, and they will go elsewhere.
- *Micromanaging.* Micromanagement makes them cranky.

- *Expecting them to report every little detail to you.* They want their independence, and they want to be measured on overall results.
- *Encroaching on what little authority you give them.* In their minds, one can never have enough authority.
- *Swaying them with emotional argument.* They equate selling with lying. No kidding.
- *Expecting them to be warm and fuzzy when working with others.* They work best by themselves.

On the other hand, the following can make Trailblazers tick:

- *Providing them with control, authority, autonomy and independence.* They will fight you for it and reward you with results when they have it.
- *Providing them with challenges.* They enjoy the game. Business is a game to most Trailblazers. The money is often just a metric, Tier IV
- *Providing them with the ability to delegate details.* They will control them anyways, so let them get it off their plates.
- *Providing them with rewards and the ability to get ahead.* They are all about results.
- *Communicating with them from a logical perspective.* They do not like being swayed by emotional argument. As soon as you start selling, they think something is wrong.

Go-Getters' Code of Conduct

Go-Getters have a high level of both dominance and sociability and are also driven and independent. Go-Getters have one thing over Trailblazers, and that is their ability to relate to others. Of course, Trailblazers probably look at that as a weakness. For the Go-Getter, it's actually a strength because they use it to their advantage. The following could tick off Go-Getters:

- *Micromanaging.* They want and need their independence and will fight for it if they don't have it.
- *Looking over their shoulders.* They want to be measured on overall results, and they get cranky if they feel micromanaged. Their attitude is "I was looking for a job when I found this one."

- *Keeping them out of the communication loop.* They have a high level of sociability, and they need that social stimulation to feel good about themselves.
- *Putting them in a position that requires a lot of repetition.* They can handle it and be good at it but only for a relatively short period of time.

The following can make Go-Getters tick:

- *Providing them the ability to set stimulating goals.* Don't be surprised if they have a tendency to go off on tangents.
- *Providing them with social stimulation.* Put them in an environment where they get to be with others.
- *Asking for and listening to their opinions.* They will give them to you anyways.
- *Allowing them to delegate the details.* They don't like them anyway.
- *Suggesting that they take on a team perspective.* Don't be too upset when they tell you that there is no "I" in TEAM.

Managers' Code of Conduct

Managers have a high level of dominance and a low level of sociability. They are more relaxed, analytical, and independent. The Managers are really pretty tough characters. They have the toughness of Trailblazers, but are much more patient. It is this factor that makes them loyal to their people. They really like to think things through, and this trait makes them appear stubborn.

The following could tick off Managers:

- *Doing everything your way.* They may have a different approach that could bring improvements.
- *Letting them get away with anything.* Hold them accountable. If you don't hold them accountable, they may lose respect for you.
- *Hesitating to speak your mind.* They may not seem open to the opinions of others, but if you ask the question, "Are you open for a suggestion?" they will actually listen.
- *Expecting them to become an instant friend.* They are relatively private people and are choosy as to whom they invite into their lives.

- *Complimenting them unnecessarily.* They are very private individuals and are not comfortable being swayed with superficialities.
- *Being put off if they come across as being a little less than diplomatic.* They are a little bit less than diplomatic.

The following can make Managers tick:

- *Urging them to delegate the details.* They can be very controlling. They know that they are tough on others, but they don't appear to care. Actually they do.
- *Allowing them to use their initiative and work independently.* They do their best work when they are working by themselves.
- *Welcoming their opinions and anticipating their willingness to be stubborn and take a stand.* (I threw that stubborn stuff to see if you are still reading. If you are a Manager, you may not have gotten it yet!)
- *Coaching them to adopt more of a team perspective.* Then get out of their way. I use the four-penny technique with Managers.
- *Minimizing deadlines/changes and explaining why you're changing something.* The Manager is quite the creature of habit, and they have difficulty embracing change.

Motivators' Code of Conduct

Motivators' have a high level of both dominance and sociability, with their sociability greater than their dominance. They are also very driven and independent. They are great at most things that have to do with relationships and the results that can come from them.

The following could tick off Motivators:

- *Assigning them too many routine, repetitive tasks.* They don't deal well with a mundane environment. They enjoy change, and they will find a way of turning a stable environment into a more exciting one (for them).
- *Dampening their excitement and enthusiasm by keeping them on track.* Sometimes their tangents pay off with expected results.

- *Objecting if they let things go to the last minute.* They work very well under pressure. (You have no idea when this is being written. I have been making my wife Renee crazy for the last several months. I work best under pressure.)
- *Being too negative and insincere, or shutting them out.* Because of their high level of sociability, they need to remain positive and be part of things.
- *Micromanaging.* They enjoy their freedom. If they want their freedom, then make a deal with them. Give them freedom in exchange for their compliance on their metrics. Manage them by numbers.

The following can make Motivators tick:

- *Allowing for a fast-changing environment.* They do some of their best work when they are allowed to go off on the occasional tangent.
- *Getting their buy-in as to setting deadlines.* Otherwise, it can be difficult to hold them accountable.
- *Building a strategy for them to stay in focus.* They know that they can be their own worst enemy, and they will usually be open for a suggestion or two.
- *Providing them with opportunities to interact with others.* Motivators enjoy working by, with and through others and use their sociability as a tool to get things done.
- *Utilizing them to help resolve any people conflicts and to get others to open up.* The challenge here is that there is also the risk that the Motivator can have difficulty keeping it professional.

Authorities Code of Conduct

Authorities are true Specialists in that they have both low levels of dominance and sociability. They are very accepting and analytical. They also have high levels of both relaxation and compliance. They will do almost anything they can to stay out of trouble, avoid confrontation, and above all, do things right. This is the personality you want for your surgeon. It is also that same personality as a traffic cop, school teacher, and an auto mechanic. Think about it the next time you are visiting with your doctor – that a great surgeon and incredible auto mechanic could share the same personality, despite their different skills, education, and experience. One probably drives a better car – the auto mechanic – and it's paid for.

The following could tick off Authorities:

- *Giving them vague instructions.* They do not deal well with ambiguity. They prefer specifics; after all, their favorite question is, "How?" How do you want this done?
- *Making them responsible for difficult people.* They prefer harmony and will avoid the tough people decisions whenever possible.
- *Expecting them to make big decisions quickly or easily.* They base their decisions on their level of expertise. If they have it, they are cool with the decisions. If they don't, then they will want to take the time to learn more about the area under discussion.
- *Expecting results before they are ready.* They can make the Authority really cranky. Remember, the Authorities kind of ruminate. They take it and take it and take it, and then they may explode. It leaves everybody else wondering where the hell that came from.
- *Becoming overly frustrated or anxious if they are too caught up in the fine points.* That kind of attention to detail can sometimes prevent mistakes. It will still make a Generalist crazy, but it becomes normal frustration if others know it is supposed to be frustrating.

The following can make Authorities tick:

- *Reaching agreement with them on their specific goals, time lines, and expectations.* Otherwise these can make Authorities really anxious. They take most things very seriously.
- *Giving them the credit they deserve.* But do your best to provide any recognition in a very professional manner, with few to no surprises.
- *Spending the time necessary to answer their questions about specific aspects of a project or task.* Remember they are real "how" people and will want to know how something should be done. The rest of their thinking is: If they know how, then they will do it right. If they do it right, then they will avoid

blame. The real challenge takes place when the Authority works for a Generalist, and at the conclusion of the project the Generalist asks the Specialist, "Why did you do it that way?" Here comes the blame!

- *Being patient.* Do be patient. Do be patient largely because Generalists have little or no choice in the manner and Authorities hate being rushed anyway.
- *Encouraging them to set up their own routines and provide flexible time frames.* This is where the Authorities are really cool. They are usually very strong creatures of habit. They have three favorite restaurants, and they almost always order the same items. You always know what to expect.

Collaborators' Code of Conduct

Collaborators differ from Authorities mainly in their sociability. They are very warm and friendly, and much more outgoing than Authorities. Collaborators have the same basic attributes as Authorities except for their higher level of sociability. Therefore, you can go ditto for most Authorities' items plus these that are attributable to the sociability factor.

The following can tick off Collaborators:

- *Shutting them out.* They feel they need to be part of things. Notice I said "feel" not "think." They are the extroverts that feel.
- *Being insincere.* They can usually accept the good and the bad in people. However, that doesn't make it any easier for them to hold others accountable.
- *Putting pressure on them.* Do this only if it is absolutely necessary, and then give them as much notice as possible. Remember, they function best in a stable, calm, predictable environment.
- *Leaving everything to the last minute.* They can handle some emergencies, especially if the task falls within their area of expertise. The challenge is that many Collaborators work with a Generalist and usually one that is driven and a natural procrastinator. This is where the Captain Chaos title for the Generalist comes from.

The following (primarily related to the sociability factor) can make Collaborators tick:

- *Including them as an integral part of your team*. They hate to be left out of things and can take it downright personally.
- *Actively soliciting their perspective in meetings and relying on their specialized focus*. Because of their sociability, they are comfortable talking in meetings, especially when it is about their areas of expertise.
- *Ensuring that they receive the credit they deserve*. This is important as they want their pats on the back.
- *Providing them with opportunities to interact with others and get their people fix*. If you are an introvert, then this will be a crazy-maker for you.
- *Making the most of their ability to communicate*. Seek their insights into people.

Diplomats' Code of Conduct

Diplomats are known to have it going on from an entrepreneurial perspective, even though they are accepting and compliant like the other Specialists. They also possess a high level of sociability and are driven. These two aspects allow them to do better in many relationship opportunities or environments.

The following can tick off Diplomats:

- *Assigning them too many routine, repetitive tasks*. They get bored quickly. They can handle the routine, but they can also put that pressure on others.
- *Becoming defensive if they constantly want to change things*. They do well under pressure and are comfortable with change.
- *Expecting results before they have finished the project*. Their through approach requires that they complete assignments fully. The good news is that asking them to hurry up works better with Diplomats than with any other Specialists.
- *Shutting them out*. They need to be in on things. They want to, and need to, be part of a team – your team.

- *Being insincere.* It hurts their feelings.

The following can make Diplomats tick:

- *Fostering a fast-changing environment and giving them a bit of rein.*
- *Involving them in setting deadlines and soliciting their agreement as to when a project or task will be done.*
- *Building a strategy for them to maintain their focus.*
- *Providing an overview of their role in relation to the whole.* They like this.
- *Providing them with opportunities to interact with others.* Remember they are usually pretty good at that teamwork stuff.

Chapter 11

-- The Bottom Line --

➢ The Golden Rule of "Do unto others as you would have them do unto you" should be changed to "Do unto others as they would have you do unto them." Treat others the way they prefer.

➢ Great leaders have an understanding of the motivational needs of others. Great leaders represent a very small percentage.

➢ Great leaders use personality assessments to objectively measure the personality of others so they know exactly how to treat them.

➢ High Dominant personalities prefer independence, control, authority, and autonomy.

➢ Those with high sociability enjoy social stimulation, recognition, and working with others.

➢ People with high levels of relaxation prefer a stable environment where they know what to expect and are rewarded for their loyalty.

➢ Highly compliant individuals like security, rules, policies, and a book to follow.

CHAPTER

12

Crossroads of

Mediocrity

AN ENTREPRENEURIAL CLIENT TOLD ME THE FOLLOWING STORY. "IN 1984, I lost it. Not my mental faculties, but my financial wherewithal. I lost it all." Actually, he joked and said, "I'm not sure exactly what my wherewithal is, so let's say I was out of money." He had been working on a foreign project for an entire year. It was his moon shot – you know – the deal that really makes a difference in your business. (I personally believe that people should only spend five to 20 percent of their time working on their moon shots, but others make different choices.) He'd followed that business deal halfway around the world only to realize that it had been a mistake. He admitted, "It was a long, lonely flight home." He said the next morning he was sitting in bed, feeling sorry for himself when he realized that he had a choice. He could either accept this path of mediocrity on his doorstep, or he could get back to work in the proverbial saddle. He chose the second option and has been going strong ever since.

Most entrepreneurial types not only have an innate urge to "get back to work," but many of them also have an inner drive to accumulate wealth and continue to increase their financial security. When I learned that 90 percent of our population retires at the age of 65, with less than $10,000 in the bank, I couldn't believe it. I acknowledge that everybody experiences challenges that affect their finances, but I also know that the outcome often has more to do with how they handle the situation than with the situation itself.

These major challenges seem to show up at least once every seven years or so. Just like the seven-year return of the locust, everyone has these experiences in life. It's as predictable as divorce, a layoff, an injury, an accident, or something that causes both consternation and questions one's core beliefs. The question is, what will you do when it happens next?

Turning Developmental Considerations into Strengths

I've worked with, coached, and provided direction to thousands of frustrated business executives and wantrepreneurs alike. These business executives usually have a strong sense of where they want to be; the good ones rarely have the patience that goes with scaling the corporate ladder. Entrepreneurs can be way too headstrong, and what they need is something to prevent them from sabotaging themselves. And, as for the wantrepreneurs, they need strong direction and a "book to go by." It's often easier to coach wantrepreneurs than executives or entrepreneurs because they're looking for structure – any structure.

For example, at the end of World War I, the purpose of the Versailles Treaty was to punish the German people by requiring them to make reparations. The country was decimated; it was basically left without an infrastructure. As you may have noticed, the German people are largely a by-the-book culture. Almost everything runs on time in a fairly structured environment. But, at the end of World War I they were left without a book to follow, so they embraced Adolf Hitler and the book Mein Kampf. (English: My Struggle or My Battle) The German people could have – perhaps would have – embraced almost any book at that time.

Self-awareness, cognitive capacity, goals, a road map to being your best, the desire to change – all phrases that look like sound bites taken from many of today's best sellers.

The difference between a sound bite and an accomplishment is actualization, being able to take direction and actualize it into achievable, measurable (Tier IV) results (Tier V).

Remember, for each behavioral strength there's a corresponding and diametrically opposed potential limitation. When I want to be politically correct, I refer to these potential limitations as developmental considerations. (Sounds nice, doesn't it?) These are the challenges experienced by every personality type. People can't help it – it's just a way of life. For example, consider these potential limitations:

- If you're very dominant and self-confident, you may not be terribly open to suggestions.
- If you're accepting and a great team player, you may find it difficult to be highly results-oriented or to hold others accountable.
- If you're highly sociable, have many friends, and work well with others, you may want to be liked at the expense of getting results.
- If you're highly analytical and great with numbers, your challenge may come from dealing with others.
- If you have a high level of relaxation and are a strong creature of habit, your challenge could be dealing with change.
- If you have a lot of drive, you may get bored easily.
- If you have a high level of compliance and prefer working with a lot of structure, you may find it difficult to work in a more free-flowing environment.
- If you're very independent and work better without strong guidance, your challenge may be working in positions requiring great attention to detail.

For example, Alexandra was a Specialist extraordinaire. More specifically, she was a Diplomat, one with very good taste. In fact, she was a phenomenal chef. A graduate of a New York culinary school, she knew her way around a kitchen. She had tremendous flair and was great with people, but she lacked a flair for numbers, the strategic vision to really know how to capitalize on her talents. She also lacked the self-confidence to open her own catering business.

After a couple years experience in the catering business, though, Alex discovered a business opportunity that had her name on it. Well, actually it had someone else's name on it, but it felt like hers. She opened a location that offered cooking lessons, "cook it in advance" food preparation, and – her real dream: catering. Fast-forward four years to

Alex's thriving business. With an ample supply of customers and a very highly performing location, Alex is great with the people, with the recipes, and with the selling. Her challenge was the Generalist side of the business. Remember the five-tier pyramid? Tier I was the core, the personality, the natural style, and Alex has a Diplomat's personality. As far as the behaviors (Tier II) required to get the job done, in Alex's case, it's the behaviors of the Go-Getter. Her actions (Tier III) consisted of the following:

- She wrote a business and marketing plan in conjunction with her SCORE consultant.
- She spoke weekly to women's clubs and provided samples.
- She offered cooking lessons as a part of silent auctions for the local schools and provided samples.
- She presented to local church and civic groups and provided samples.
- She advertised in the local newspapers and magazines, and provided samples to their staff.
- She passed out flyers to neighborhood businesses and provided samples.
- She offered her location for meetings to the local Chamber of Commerce and provided samples.
- She sent samples and invitations to people listed in her weekly newspaper as recently engaged, setting the stage for future wedding orders.
- She sent congratulation baskets of samples to new businesses.
- And, she worked her behind off, night and day, every day for two years.

The bottom line is that Alex made and gave away a ton of samples, and today she has a very successful business. She did whatever it took, and today she has a salesperson, a staff, and more press than Napa Valley during the autumn crush. Most recently, Alex received a very nice offer from a company that wants to buy her business. It is not the exit strategy she is looking for. She wants to have her own line of retail products and to publish a catering book before she will consider offers. So, to date her results (Tier V) have been excellent. By the way, Alex measured her actions (Tier IV) every step of the way.

Alex's example shows what a Specialist is able to do with the right plan of action. The Generalist is certainly cut from a different cloth, but he achieves the same results. Take Hal Mitchell. Hal lived in the Midwest and became the reluctant owner of a family candy business. Hal wasn't planning on taking over or even working in the family business, but when his father took ill, he dropped out of school and did just that. The company had been managed by a master candy maker, and it was Hal's job to make something of the business. While in college, Hal had held several part-time sales positions, and he was good, very good.

Hal's Achilles' heel was that he knew nothing about the candy business and his livelihood was in the hands of the hired help. He felt as if he were being held hostage and, in a sense, he was. He had the Tier I covered – as he had a Go-Getter personality. He had most of the Tier II covered – in that he knew what he needed for success. And, his action (Tier III) consisted of the following:

- He had no business plan, only a sense of what he wanted to do. Soon after joining the company, he attended a candy school in Philadelphia and he was able to become a pretty decent candy maker in a matter of weeks.
- He came in on weekends and practiced making candy.
- He began selling and opened a number of accounts at nearby truck stops. In his first year, he opened more than 100 accounts.
- He placed product announcements in a national hotel magazine.
- He began providing candy amenities to a number of hotels.
- He fired his master candy maker.
- He bought the equipment necessary for automation.
- He contracted with a private-label candy company to make his product, and he became a pure marketing organization.
- He built his business, eventually sold it to take care of his family and later bought another business.

One Generalist, one Specialist -- similar results.

Goal Orientation and Motivation

Being a highly successful entrepreneur requires a high level of motivation. Here are some ways to improve your motivation:

- Give yourself a taste of success to develop faith in the worthiness of your goals. For example, if you'd like to start a career helping people in some way, volunteer somewhere to gain experience. If you want to write a novel, begin with a short story.

Once you experience a "slice" of your goal, you'll be more driven to pursue it outright.

- Get a mentor. Do you know someone inspiring? Learn what you can from his experience.
- Consider that poorly chosen goals may decrease your motivation. Ponder questions such as: Are your goals realistic? Are they really what you care about or do they represent other people's ambitions for you? Try to find a goal that's realistic *and* that motivates you.
- Are other things going on in your life that could be depleting your motivation? If you're stressed or dealing with major issues, it may be hard to even think about goals. Take care of these issues, and your drive should improve.
- Apply self-control and self-discipline. Practice delaying gratification and stifling impulsiveness.
- Take small steps if the big ones overwhelm you. So, if your goal is to sell a new idea at work, take care of all the details first. Gather information, take the preliminary steps, and watch the project take on a life of its own. Reward yourself when you complete different steps.
- Make contracts with yourself. Write down the reasons you want to pursue a goal, and refer to it later when you feel discouraged.
- Learn to be your own coach. Practice positive self-talk, and give yourself a pat on the back.
- Post your goals somewhere prominent so you can see them every day.

Emotional Expression

Emotional expression is a critical aspect of emotional intelligence – a necessary component for successful entrepreneurs. Here are some ways to improve your ability to express emotions:

- Take small steps. Start expressing emotions that are the least intimidating; and you'll find that it's not as bad as you think. On the positive side, begin with genuine compliments, and then take it further to an expression of appreciation. When you need to communicate a negative feeling, try writing it if you feel too intimidated to say it. Like any new skill it gets easier with practice.

- Choose what's most important. Obviously you can't express every little feeling or be particularly emotional toward someone. It's more effective (and healthier) to pace your expressions evenly. Don't wait for the floodgates to open, because they can't hold up any longer.
- Learn to communicate effectively. An important factor in the effectiveness of expressing emotions is *how* we do it. Blowing up at someone, for example, is usually not the best way to communicate a feeling. Good communication skills are key. And being skills, they can be learned.
- Build self-confidence and self-esteem. The more confident you become, the easier it should be to express your feelings.
- Build meaningful, trusting relationships. Most people need someone they can talk to, someone to whom they can express their feelings without fear of rejection or ridicule.
- Consider the implications of not releasing your feelings; lack of intimacy with others, pent-up emotions, health problems, etc.
- Remember that communication involves a lot more than what is spoken. Your gestures, expressions, and tone of voice send signals that are just as strong as (or even stronger than) the words you choose.
- Practice distinguishing between what you're thinking and what you're feeling. They're not always one and the same, and you need to recognize this in order to clearly express yourself.

Social Insight and Empathy

Being able to accurately assess people's opinions and emotions gives entrepreneurs an edge. Here are some ideas for increasing one's social insight and empathy:

- Pay attention to how others react and what they communicate to you. Putting in the extra effort to really listen and observe can teach you a lot about human interaction and emotions.
- While you certainly can't fake empathy, you can increase your connection to other people by truly listening and trying to put yourself in their shoes.
- Build meaningful relationships that teach you about human nature.

- If you're not sure how someone is feeling, ask for clarification (if it's appropriate). A simple "How are you feeling?" or "Would you explain your perspective to me?" might do the trick.
- Put aside your own preoccupations to consider what might be going through other people's minds in different situations. Ask yourself how you'd feel in a similar situation. Try to identify at least two or three angles from which to see it. Put empathy into action. Get involved in helping people in some way (e.g. volunteering). The closer you get to a situation, the more you should realize the difficulties others might be facing. Remember, in every situation there are several perspectives.

Stranger than Fiction

Twenty-five years ago I ran the following ad in The Wall Street Journal: "Thirty-five-year-old entrepreneur with strong corporate background seeks mentor who owns business, has no children to leave it to, and desires to retire and stay involved. To my surprise, I received about 20 calls, many of which were excellent opportunities. Unfortunately, I didn't feel passionate about any of them. They were all older business owners who had created high levels of net worth and had successfully put their children through college. Their children had become professionals and weren't interested in continuing the family business. There's a strong similarity between the responses I got and the responses of those reported in *The Millionaire Next Door*. It was the business owner's goal to provide an education sufficient to guarantee that the child wouldn't need to go into the family business. And they did not.

To win, it becomes essential for the entrepreneur and the wantrepreneur alike to understand how their own stupid switches affect them; specifically, how the switch can be turned on and off. What causes you to react? What physical manifestations take place about three seconds before you blow your cool? Not sure? Ask your kids – they know. They might say, "Oh Daddy gets those little lines between his eyes, and he starts to breathe really, really deeply." Learn this, and control your destiny.

Chapter 12

— The Bottom Line —

➢ Most entrepreneurial types not only have an innate urge to "get back to work," but many also have an inner drive to accumulate wealth and continue to increase their financial security.

➢ Most entrepreneurs go years without needing a sick day and yet they're frustrated because they have employees that can't string 30 days of work together without missing one of them.

➢ Major challenges seem to show up at least once every seven years or so. The question is, "What will you do when it happens next?"

➢ For every behavioral strength, there is a corresponding and diametrically opposed potential limitation.

➢ Understanding five-tier thinking brings you closer to achieving your goals.

➢ Beat the odds through a heightened level of self-awareness.

➢ The Four-Penny Technique increases our sociability. Start each day with four pennies in your right pocket. Your job is to have four positive conversations with four different employees each day (Tier III, actions). With each compliment we move a penny from one pocket to the other (Tier IV, metrics). This drives positive morale throughout the organization. Oh yeah. You can't end a compliment with the word "but."

➢ There are a number of CEO or entrepreneur peer groups. For a list of organizations and links go to www.ceoexpress.com.

➢ Most entrepreneurs use their own form of a five-tier pyramid, but they do so subconsciously. The key to the Five-Tier Performance Pyramid is doing so cognitively, consciously, *and* objectively.

CHAPTER

13

The Goldilocks Theory

Creating an Organization That's Just Right

GOLDILOCKS WENT FOR A WALK ONE DAY AND PRETTY SOON, SHE CAME UPON A house. She knocked and when no one answered she went in. At the kitchen table there were three bowls of porridge. Given that Goldilocks was very hungry, she tasted one bowl of porridge, but it was too hot. The second bowl was too cold. But the third bowl was just right and she ate it happily. I'm sure you know the rest of the story. However, was this really a fairy tale, or was it more like a fable with organizational development implications?

Imagine that Goldilocks was an entrepreneur looking to assemble the perfect team. Some applicants were too strong, some were not strong enough, and some were just right. Or, what about looking for that perfect opportunity? Some were too expensive, some were too mundane, and some were just right. Short of a fairy tale and the guaranteed happy ending, how can we tell which employee opportunity is *just right*?

The essence of this work is measuring those qualities that are typically the most important to measure. Unfortunately, they are also the most neglected and most difficult to measure.

My wife, Renee, and I co-founded our firm some 20+ years ago. We have a great team; Goldilocks would be proud. But if you can't get it right in our business using our tools, then something is wrong. The past several years have generated a number of interesting projects. They included a scoring exercise, where we identified challenges, recommended solutions, implemented our ideas, and measured our results. Here are a few of these challenges, their solutions, and their results.

Situation and Challenge 1

Job-Fit

A benchmark study published by the *Harvard Business Review* looked at the relationship between performance, age, gender, race/color, education, experience, and personality. The research question was, "Who would make the best salesperson?" More than 1,500 salespeople working in 14 different industries were surveyed. Seven were high-turnover industries such as automobile and insurance sales. Seven were low-turnover industries, such as pharmaceutical and heavy equipment sales. The study differentiated the results into four groups; 1st quartile, 2nd quartile, 3rd quartile, and 4th quartile. The 1st quartile represented the top 25 percent performance. When looking at the performance of those who reached the first quartile, the study authors found there was only a 1 percent differential between men and women, between those over 40 and those under 40, between Caucasians and people of color, between those with experience and those without, and between those with college degrees and those without. There was, however, an 18 percent differential between those with the right personalities for the job and those without. The researchers referred to this matching as "job-fit".

If you recall the Five-Tier Pyramid, having the right personality represents the concept of job-fit, matching the personality of the individual with the behavioral requirements of the position.

Notice the percentage associated with those that either quit or were fired. The majority of those who left did so during the first six months when the cost of turnover is lower. But still, the cost of losing a good salesperson can be in the tens of thousands of dollars. Even losing a bad salesperson can be expensive. If you would like to have a formula for determining the cost of turnover, please go to www.accordmanagementsystems.com. Turnover cost for sales and executive positions can cost a company more than 100 percent of the position's annual salary.

The Best Salespeople

Months Hiring	Performance Quartile				Quit/after Fired
	1st	2nd	3rd	4th	
6-month/job-fit	11%	26%	23%	14%	24%
6-month/no job-fit	2%	10%	18%	24%	48%
14-month/job-fit	19%	42%	7%	4%	28%
14-month/no job-fit	1%	6%	14%	22%	57%

*Due to rounding there is a slight difference

Source: *Harvard Business Review*, July/August, 1985

Situation and Challenge 2

A master franchisee in the quick lube industry owned 14 locations. He knew he didn't have the right people on the proverbial bus. He had lower bay technicians who forgot to replace oil pan plugs correctly. He had cashiers who felt that selling was a form of lying. He had managers whose nature caused too many employees to quit. The owner of the franchise had a Manager personality and, in spite of this, his company serviced upwards of 1,000 cars per day.

My firm, Accord Management Systems measured the behavioral requirements of each and every position. We found the behavioral requirement of a lower bay technician was an Authority personality. Upper bay technician could either be Authorities or Collaborators. Their sociability would come in handy as they sometimes covered the register when the cashier was on break. The cashier should be a Diplomat, and the assistant manager should be a Go-Getter or a Motivator. The last two would be best because of their levels of sociability, which were imperative in terms of selling and retaining customers. This is what Goldilocks had in mind. In reality, the personalities of store managers and cashiers were mainly way too gruff. They believed selling was just wrong. In fact, when we started working with this company only 15 percent of their employees possessed the right personalities (Tier I) for their positions (Tier II). The existing employees knew technically what to do which included knowing what kind of oil to use, the thickness of brake pad, and the warranty on wiper blades.

Figure 13.1: **Master Franchise Case Study-Employee Job-Fit**

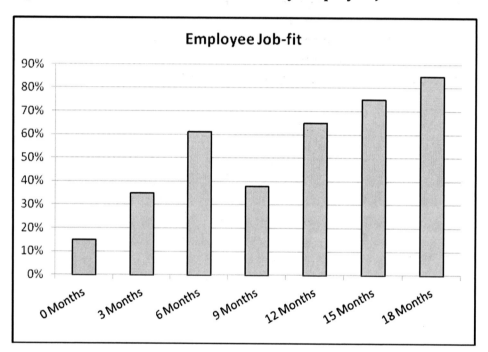

The above graph shows how we were able to move forward in job-fit. You will notice there was a setback in the acquisition of the right talent between the sixth and ninth month. This was due to the fact that management promoted a number of better employees to training and quality assurance positions. The company also implemented a 90-day probationary policy for new hires, and there were a number of new hires that despite their apparent fit weren't performing well enough. They were terminated.

Once the new teams were in place, the management team also added the right training and expectations. The expectations also included the right metrics (Tier IV) so that each store knew how it was doing every day, week, and month. They embraced the theory that if you can't measure it, you can't manage it, so they did both.

FIGURE 13.2: **Master Franchisee Case Study – Sales Increase**

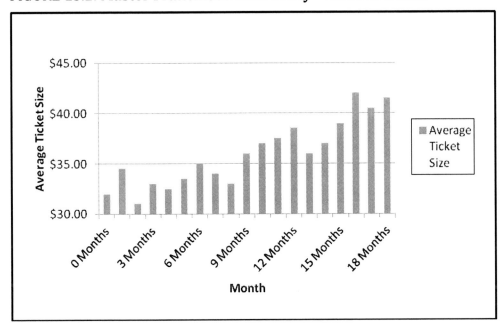

The above figure shows how sales increased as employee job fit improved. That's right. The company wrote an average of 1,000 tickets per day and by the end of the 18-month case study, it was able to increase average ticket size by over $6 per ticket. That adds up to additional annual revenues of $2,160,000. For the most part, that occurred without increasing the largest line item: employee cost.

This is a proof statement. If you measure the behavioral requirements of each and every position and hire against those benchmarks, you will be able to determine what each seat on the bus requires and place the right people in the right seats. These are results (Tier V). The cost of implementation for a company with 14 locations, 300+ employees is about $10,000. If you spent $10,000 and received a return on an additional $2,160,000, then your ROI is phenomenal.

Situation and Challenge 3

A client, a buying group of home improvement materials, was transitioning from a buying group to a franchise. They had thousands of members. Each was highly independent. Store signs tended to be personal, like Bob's Flooring. Its challenge was to have the signs read: "FRANCHISE NAME" in big letters with "Bob's Flooring" in smaller lettering, thereby creating a stronger brand. We created a Franchise Engagement Survey, which included 70 questions and several demographic questions. The demographics included "tenure", "plans on moving and when," and "plans to remodel and when."

We discovered that 32 percent of their members were planning on either moving or remodeling within the next three years. The owners of the company had not been aware of this but saw it as a definite opportunity. They created a branding initiative in the form of a new sign that was paid for by the franchisor. The franchisee got a new sign paid for by someone else, and the franchisor got the consistency it wanted. Had it not asked the right questions, it would have missed a tremendous opportunity.

Situation and Challenge 4

A Midwest Manufacturer was concerned about its level of employee engagement. Employee engagement is a measure of employee satisfaction. Engaged employees are three times more productive than are disengaged employees. We designed an engagement survey. It measured the employees' engagement (feelings) about how they perceived treatment by their supervisors, management, and senior management. We measure 14 major areas that encompassed more than 65 questions and responses.

We discovered the manufacturer had an aging workforce, which wasn't either a surprise or a problem. The problem was that 27 percent of this aging workforce was planning on retiring five years sooner than the manufacturer had anticipated. This new information gave the manufacturer the opportunity to look at employees with the right personalities to move up within the organization. In essence, it allowed the company to get the right people on the bus *and* to provide them with the right training. It also allowed the company to be proactive and to create solutions before the problems became noticeable.

Situation and Challenge 5

A franchisor dealing in early childhood education was frustrated because its franchisees were performing at different levels. The franchisees all paid the same franchisee fee; all had virtually identical build outs and all had the same training. So what was the problem? We surveyed the personalities of its 250 franchisees. We segmented these surveys based on performance. We also created a franchise engagement survey that included 45 questions designed to determine franchisee level of engagement. Did they like what they were doing? Did they like the decision they made to buy into this opportunity?

We discovered there was a direct relationship between engagement of the franchisee, the personality of the franchisee, and the royalties generated by the franchisee. The optimum profile was that of Trailblazers with slightly higher levels of sociability. They generated $52,000 in annual royalties. This means they generated more than $600,000 in annual revenues, of which the franchisee got to keep 92 percent, or $552,000.

But what if the franchisee did not have a Trailblazer personality? They made less. To solve this, the franchisor created a training program for all its franchisees that showed them the behaviors (Tier II) and the actions (Tier III) necessary to be more successful. Ultimately, many of these franchisees delivered better results (Tier VI).

FIGURE 13.3: **Engagement and Personality Survey of Leading Franchisor**

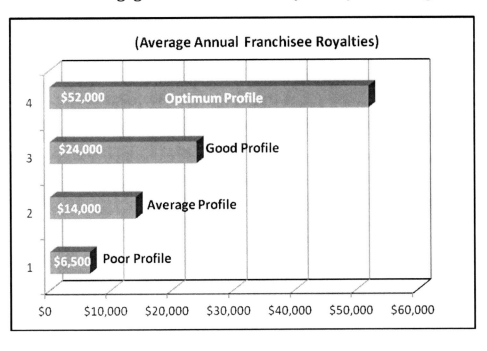

FIGURE 13.4: **Personalities Involved with Each Accomplishment**
The Program

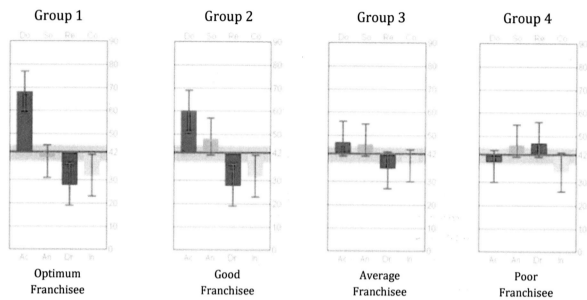

The position of franchisee was a combination of teacher, store manager, and store-owner. The franchisor determined what the right Tier II: Behaviors were for the position. They are listed below with the personality factor listed in italics:

1. Very competitive, ambitious, and goal-oriented *(Dominance)*
2. Wants responsibility for and authority over others *(Dominance)*
3. Enjoys overcoming objections/resistance and achieving goals in the face of obstacles *(Dominance)*
4. Restless, driving, and energetic *(Drive)*
5. Sense of urgency to get things done quickly*(Independence)*
6. Works well under pressure and deadline *(Drive)*
7. Independent and persistent *(Independence)*
8. Wants to take charge and show initiative *(Independence)*
9. A balance between people and a work orientation *(Sociability)*
10. Works well with people, yet does not require a lot of social or people stimulation *(Sociability)*

The training program determined a number of Tier III: Actions, that when acted upon, eventually lead to better Tier V: Results. The actions were:

1. Called on local schools and day care facilities and discussed the franchise education programs and how they support the curriculum of teachers.
2. Offered and sponsored a number of programs that were community-oriented in order to get her name into the market.
3. Purchased mailing lists that included residents within a three-mile radius. This list was sorted to include only those homes with children.
4. Spoke almost weekly to various civic groups about the Center's programming. At each stop she offered a free day-pass.
5. Developed a birthday program and marketed it through schools, day care facilities, and church groups.

The franchisees were able to increase their student count within 120 days of successful implementation of the above actions. Not all franchisees chose to participate.

Situation and Challenge 6

One client, a telemarketing organization, had watched its sales plummet over the previous six months. They reviewed their hiring system to check for flaws. Its interview process began with the human resources manager conducting an initial screening interview. From there, second and final interviews were conducted by the telemarketing manager. We consulted with the firm in order to determine its status and to address any problems. We discovered that the personality required for new employees was that of a Diplomat. The telemarketing manager had a Go-Getter personality, but the real kicker was that the new HR manager was an Authority.

Fulfill Your Expectations

We have tested and tested and tested. We have surveyed and surveyed. And each and every time the results have been what we expected. We've learned about the people side of the business. We've learned that we can predict what is going to happen. And if we can predict it – guess what – we can change it, make it better, or just celebrate in our wisdom.

Actually, we aren't' that wise, but we have learned. We learned that if you first measure the behavioral requirement of the position and then hire with that benchmark in mind, the odds of that person performing the way you want are pretty good. We can tell you 90 percent of the time who can't do a job; the other 10 percent, you will have to figure out on your own. It's not that tough when you have removed the wrong 90 percent.

The company actually needed an HR manager who was a Diplomat or a Collaborator. It wanted someone with sociability, and it got someone who was very analytical and believed that selling was tantamount to lying. Because of this, whenever applicants with higher levels of sociability began selling themselves, the HR manager developed an immediate dislike for them. The only applicants who reached the second interview were introverts. The telemarketing manager did the best he could with those he interviewed; but, unfortunately, it wasn't good enough. Once the company was able to determine the challenge by the introverted HR manager and began to utilize personality testing, it was able to turn around its operation within 30 days. That is the power of being able to measure the operation (Tier IV).

Situation and Challenge 7

A client was trying to determine which personality type would be best for the position of store manager – a Generalist or a Specialist. It looked at performance levels of these two personality types. After looking at hundreds of data points, the client found that the sales generated by Generalists (over the first six months in their positions) were 32 percent greater than the results generated by Specialists.

Now what?

I invite you to go to our corporate website for the latest in survey results and a list of other applications that can be utilized with the right test survey. If you're a business owner or a member of "C Level," then send us an e-mail requesting to take the same survey used as part of this research. You will be invited to take a behavioral survey that will provide you with additional insights about yourself and the business decisions you'll make in the future.

The web site is constantly updated, and once you've taken your first survey, you'll be invited to take others. I know you'll find this to be both of interest and value. If you register for our newsletter, you'll receive updates, discounts, products and services, and, perhaps most importantly, literally thousands of dollars in value. You will have the opportunity to take an Entrepreneurial Test. This will help you determine what you want to be when you grow up. Go to www.theentrepeneurnextdoor.com to register.

Why do we offer this complimentary service? Fair question. We do this because either you already own a business or someday you'll own a business. At some point you'll need a company to help you get the people side of the business right. Then, perhaps you'll contact us at www.accordmanagementsystem.com.

During the thirteen years I've been associated with the CEO organization, Vistage, 15 of us have convened monthly to, as I put it, "lie to each other about how well we're doing." Our morning consists of a speaker covering a particular topic; our afternoon is spent discussing our most pressing issues, 90 percent of which are people issues. When a member raises an issue, he takes about 10 minutes to present it, including what he expects to gain from our discussion. At this point, the rest of us ask questions aimed at sharing our insights, ideas, and potential solutions. My advantage is my training and understanding of the concept discussed in this book. It's like playing a game: "I can solve this problem in five questions." Get the idea? Because of my training, I ask more behaviorally-oriented questions. When we digest this information with an overall understanding of the team in question, we can determine a plan of action. The answer to almost every question you may have about positions, employees, or yourself is available in preceding pages.

Your next steps are:

1. Determine who you are (Tier I). Are you a Generalist or a Specialist? If Specialist, are you a Diplomat, a Collaborator, or an Authority? Then study your favorite subject: yourself. Generalists get to do this, too; you just don't need to be told because you don't listen anyway.
2. Determine the qualities of the position you are in or want to be in. What you're looking for are the behaviors the position requires (Tier II). Does the job require you to be more aggressive or accommodating? It's essential that you determine what the job requires. The next step is to look at the gap between who you are and who you need to be. This gap represents the hard work ahead of you.
3. Determine the actions that will support your endeavor (Tier III). This becomes a specific action plan that involves, to say the least, action. If you are buying or investing in a business, see how much of Tier II or Tier III it provides you. If it doesn't provide much, then you might want to consider looking elsewhere. Tier III involves marketing, meeting, and doing the things that move you toward your goal.
4. Make sure you're measuring the right items; otherwise how will you know if you are growing in the right direction (Tier IV)?
5. Reap the results (Tier V).

And, as we know, it's all about the results. I wish you well.

About the Author

FOR MORE THAN 20 YEARS, BILL WAGNER, CSP HAS BEEN AT THE FOREFRONT OF entrepreneurial practice and research.

He has devoted nearly all his adult life to understanding entrepreneurs and entrepreneurship – first as a student, then as an entrepreneur, and now as an expert.

Bill is the co-founder and CEO of Accord Management Systems, Inc., a firm dedicated to helping executives draw logical conclusions about themselves and the people within their organization. Working hand-in-hand with entrepreneur-focused organizations such as Vistage, the Young Entrepreneur's Organization (YEO), and the International Franchise Association (IFA), Wagner is able to stay on the cutting edge of all things entrepreneurial.

He is an expert in due diligence, mergers and acquisitions, organizational alignment, succession planning, and tactical applications such as selection, leadership development, motivation, and team building. He helps audiences and clients understand why issues exist, what to do about them, and how to fix them. Bill refers to himself as an "insultant" rather than a mere consultant, and believes the difference is in the message. He rocks the boat by telling the truth, helping clients become their own organizational therapists. He focuses more on questioning answers than answering questions.

Unlike other organizational specialists, Bill focuses exclusively on using behavioral tools from a strategic, rather than a tactical perspective. As a result, he is one of the most in-demand authorities on the subject today. Each year, Wagner presents to thousands of CEOs at more than 100 seminars and workshops across the country. Well over 90 percent of those who hear him speak are entrepreneurs, CEOs, or C-suite executives. Widely published, his articles and interviews have appeared in such publications as: *Inc., California CEO, Workforce, Wells Fargo's Business Advisor, Handbook of Business Strategy, Lodging and Hospitality, Federal Credit Union, Los Angeles Business Journal, Franchise World, Franchise Times, Franchise Update, The Wall Street Journal, Entrepreneur,* and *EO's Axis.*

Prior to co-founding Accord Management Systems, Wagner held corporate positions at Xerox, Frito-Lay, and Protection One Alarms. A graduate of Bradley University, he resides in Westlake Village, California, with his wife and co-founder of Accord Management Systems Inc., Renee, and their three children, Alex, Rebecca, and Josh.

CPSIA information can be obtained at www.ICGtesting.com
Printed in the USA
BVOW080017060213

312491BV00004B/8/P

9 780985 864903